CHAMPIONS OF FREEDOM

The Ludwig von Mises Lecture Series

Hillsdale College Press

CHAMPIONS OF FREEDOM
The Ludwig von Mises Lecture Series—Volume 39
The Great Society

©2012 Hillsdale College Press, Hillsdale, Michigan 49242

First printing 2012

The views expressed in this volume are not necessarily the views of
Hillsdale College.

Printed in the United States of America

Front cover: President Lyndon B. Johnson, seated next to former President
Harry S Truman, signing the Medicare bill in Independence, Missouri,
on July 30, 1965.

Yoichi Okamoto, photographer — © Corbis

Library of Congress Control Number: 2011945334

ISBN 978-0-916308-35-3

Contents

JONAH GOLDBERG

From Kennedy's Myth to Johnson's Dream

Where to begin with John F. Kennedy? It is tempting to say that never has a man of such modest historical stature cast such a long shadow. But that probably gives short shrift to a lot of people. Consider Gavrilo Princip, the man who started World War One. Or Guenter Schabowsky, the East German functionary who, without authority or intent, accidentally announced that the Berlin Wall would be opened "immediately," causing a flood of events that could not be contained. Or Lee Harvey Oswald, the Communist sap who murdered JFK.

Measured on the scale of presidential greatness, John Fitzgerald Kennedy's accomplishments were sparse. But, by definition, a president of the United States is consequential because he leads *the* indispensible nation. And JFK did live in interesting times.

In terms of public policy, the Democratic Party has been a cargo cult to the New Deal for nearly 80 years. But in terms of style, it remains John Kennedy's party. JFK has been the object of liberalism's unrequited infatuation for two generations.

In 1983, on the twentieth anniversary of the Kennedy assassination, Gary Hart told *Esquire*, "If you rounded us [Democratic politicians] all up and asked, 'Why did you get into politics?' nine out of ten would say John Kennedy."

In 1988 Michael Dukakis was convinced that he was the reincar-
nation of Kennedy, even tapping Lloyd Bentsen as his running mate
to recreate the "magic" of the Boston–Austin axis.

In 1992 the high-water mark of the Clinton campaign was a
Riefenstahlesque film of a teenage Bill Clinton shaking hands with President Kennedy. Later, when Clinton confessed and apologized for the
Monica Lewinsky scandal, he asked his cabinet if anyone had a problem
with what he did. Donna Shalala, to her credit, spoke up, and he shot
back that by her standard JFK would have lost to Richard Nixon. Since
that is a fate too horrible for anyone to contemplate, no one else dared
venture a criticism. (Funny how 30 years of feminist progress can be
thrown over the side at the mere mention of Nixon's name.)

In 2004 Howard Dean and John Edwards claimed to be the true
heirs of the Kennedy mantle. John Kerry was obsessed with JFK. He
adopted a Kennedy accent in school, went by the initials JFK, and tried
to model his political career on Kennedy's.

In the 2008 presidential election, Hillary Clinton claimed she was
the real JFK in the race. But in the primary contest, as well as in the
presidential race, it was Barack Obama who won out. Comparisons to
Kennedy were frequent, though they probably took a back seat to all
the talk that Obama was a new FDR or Lincoln.

As Bill Voegeli noted in the *Claremont Review of Books*, one reason
the comparisons to Obama weren't as pronounced is that they were so
obvious. As with Kennedy, Obama is a Harvard man, young, articu-
late, "cool," with an attractive wife and two adorable children. He was
more famous for the books he had written than for his scant legislative
accomplishments. (Although in fairness to Obama, he can at least plau-
sibly claim he wrote his own books.) President Obama not only seemed
to personify the "cool pragmatism" of the Kennedy administration, he
seemed to reinvigorate America with his youth and idealism.

Myth vs. Reality

If it seems I am being unfair to Kennedy, it is not intentional. In truth, I
am being far less unfair to the man than many of his fans and would-be
heirs have been. For all of Kennedy's faults, he was the kind of Democrat
Republicans can admire. He was a fierce, even reckless, Cold Warrior.

He was a Keynesian, but of the sort who cut taxes rather than simply hurling cash at a problem. He was a patriot, even a bit of a nationalist, but also an internationalist.

In many respects he wasn't even a liberal, at least not as we understand the term today. Ted Sorensen recalled that JFK "never identified himself as a liberal; it was only after his death that they began to claim him as one of theirs."

But there is one way in which Kennedy was an exemplary liberal: his faith in experts. He was brilliant at exciting national passions, at giving grandiloquent speeches about idealism and generational passion. But behind a desk, Kennedy believed that statecraft was too important a task to leave up to the little people. Addressing a White House conference on the economy in May 1962, Kennedy spoke of the "difference between myth and reality":

> Most of us are conditioned for many years to have a political viewpoint—Republican or Democratic, liberal, conservative, moderate. The fact of the matter is that most of the problems, or at least many of them, that we now face are technical problems, are administrative problems. They are very sophisticated judgments which do not lend themselves to the great sort of "passionate movements" which have stirred this country so often in the past.

The next month in a Yale commencement address he repeated the point:

> What is at stake in our economic decisions today is not some grand warfare of rival ideologies which will sweep the country with passion but the practical management of a modern economy. What we need is not labels and clichés but more basic discussion of the sophisticated and technical questions involved in keeping a great economic machinery moving ahead.

It seems Kennedy would have as little use for the Tea Parties as Obama does.

Again as Bill Voegeli notes, even the Peace Corps, a crown jewel of Kennedy-era liberalism, was an extension of this same mindset. Average Americans don't have much know-how to offer here in the states, but in the jungles of Borneo they could do a lot of good explaining the basics of hygiene and sanitation.

Far more emblematic of Kennedy liberalism, however, was the Apollo space program. Put a bunch of experts in a room, pour money over their heads until they are nearly drowning in it, and—voila!—you can accomplish anything.

But here we should return to Lee Harvey Oswald—the loser who changed the world. James Piereson's phenomenal book *Camelot and the Cultural Revolution: How the Assassination of John F. Kennedy Shattered American Liberalism* covers this material far better than I could here, or than I did in my own book. But in short, Lee Harvey Oswald was a pro-Castro Communist disciple of Che Guevara. He killed Kennedy because Kennedy was a committed Cold War liberal anti-Communist.

To call this inconvenient to American liberalism is an understatement on the order of saying the protests in Egypt are inconvenient to Hosni Mubarek. But thanks in no small part to the fact that in 1963 the Internet did not exist, those controlling the commanding heights of the culture were capable of constructing a myth in plain sight of the nation and the world.

Jackie Kennedy, probably the chief architect of this effort, summarized her biases well when she lamented, "He didn't even have the satisfaction of being killed for civil rights.... It's—it had to be some silly little communist. It...robs his death of any meaning."

Hence Mrs. Kennedy and her abettors set to work convincing the country that Kennedy was killed by the "climate of hate" in America. Specifically, this meant opponents of civil rights, conservatives, Republicans, and so on. Nearly everyone marched in lockstep to the tune of Jackie's drum. The Chief Justice of the U.S. Supreme Court, the Pope, the *New York Times* editorial page, and all of Kennedy's eulogizers insisted that he had been killed because he symbolized not just the cause of civil rights, but of all that could be good—but wasn't—about America.

Arthur Schlesinger's one-thousand-page history of the Kennedy administration, *A Thousand Days*, doesn't even mention Lee Harvey Oswald by name. But it does go on at great length about the "climate of hate." William Manchester compared the climate in Texas to that of the Weimar republic before the Nazis came to power. A young CBS reporter,

Dan Rather, overruled by his local superiors, went over their heads to the New York office and reported as fact an untrue story that Texas school children had cheered the news that Kennedy had been killed.

"The irony of the President's death," wrote *New York Times* columnist James Reston, "is that his short administration was devoted almost entirely to various attempts to curb this very streak of violence in the American character."

This was, of course, absolute nonsense. But it didn't matter. Again and again, it was pounded into the American people that, contrary to all evidence, Kennedy had been a martyr to the civil rights crusade— when in fact he was a martyr to the anti-Communist cause.

A mere three-and-a-half hours before he died, Kennedy was boasting to the Fort Worth Chamber of Commerce that he had increased defense spending on a massive scale, including a 600 percent increase on counterinsurgency special forces in South Vietnam. The previous March, Kennedy had asked Congress to spend fifty cents of every federal dollar on defense. But again, that didn't matter. America was going with the myth, not the reality.

Even the Rolling Stones got into the act. Remember these lines from "Sympathy for the Devil": "I shouted out, 'Who killed the Kennedys?'/When after all, it was you and me." (For the record, Robert Kennedy wasn't killed for civil rights either, but for his support of Israel during the Six-Day War.)

This sentiment, Psieron persuasively argues, ultimately shattered American liberalism. JFK was too good for America, so "Amerika" killed JFK.

It didn't take long for Kennedy's entourage to fuel ever more conspiratorial conjectures that JFK had been killed not only because of civil rights but because he was going to pull the United States out of Vietnam, a theory popularized by Oliver Stone's film *JFK*.

LBJ and The Great Society

Despite his resentment of the Kennedys, the JFK myth suited President Johnson's purposes on a number of fronts. The first was getting elected president in his own right. JFK had liked and respected Barry Goldwater and had looked forward to debating him. LBJ, however, had little interest in debates. He wanted to destroy Goldwater and delegitimize his message of limited government.

It is worth recalling that LBJ was the only New Dealer to serve as president, other than Harry Truman. He saw in Kennedy's death an opportunity to complete the unfinished business of the New Deal.

His aides, at least some of them, sought something more: to make America as good as Kennedy. One of those aides was Richard Goodwin, a golden boy of the Kennedy administration. He had graduated first in his class at Harvard law, and had come to JFK's attention for his work as a congressional investigator probing the quiz show scandals of the 1950s.

LBJ had inherited Goodwin as a speechwriter. In the summer of 1965 Goodwin offered what the *New York Times* called "the most sophisticated and revealing commentary to date" on the question, What is the Great Society? His answer lay in the need for the state to give "meaning" to individuals and "make the world a more enjoyable and above all enriching place to live in." "The Great Society," Goodwin explained, "is concerned not with the quantity of our goods but the quality of our lives."

Johnson had railed, "We will do all these things because we love people instead of hate them...because you know it takes a man who loves his country to build a house instead of a raving, ranting demagogue who wants to tear down one. Beware of those who fear and doubt and those who rave and rant about the dangers of progress."

> Americans are not presented with a choice of parties. Americans are not presented with a choice of liberalism and conservatism. Americans are faced with a concerted bid for power by factions which oppose all that both parties have supported. It is a choice between the center and the fringe, between the responsible mainstream of American experience and the reckless and rejected extremes of American life.

Love versus hate, good versus evil, crazy versus sane: These were the terms LBJ and his administration set for the American people in the wake of the Kennedy assassination. And it worked. In fact, liberals have never abandoned seeing the world in such Manichean terms.

In 1964, LBJ won over Goldwater in a landslide. Moreover he effectively delegitimized conservative opposition to the Great Society and liberalism. All that remained were the liberals and the left.

For a while, the liberals believed they had it all well in hand. They were the experts. They knew what to do, just as Kennedy had said. But it turned out that what the new experts lacked wasn't simply enough data, but enough spine. They had the courage of their convictions when it came to confronting their opponents on the right, but they were helpless before their "friends" on the left. When confronted by rioters and radicals, they simply caved. Those who didn't eventually came to be known as "neoconservatives."

Liberals believe sincerely that they act out of love for their fellow man; in their arrogance they believe they have the expertise to make you worthy of their love.

President Obama is fond of the tiresome expression, "if we could put a man on the moon, we can do…" X, Y or Z. In his 2011 State of the Union Address, he returned to his claim that this is our "sputnik moment." This is a ludicrous formulation that says we desperately need to be more like China—where experts rule—in order to stay competitive. This was reminiscent of both JFK and LBJ. As Johnson explained, Sputnik fueled the war on poverty as well.

The real problem here is that the space program isn't a useful analogue to every worthwhile human endeavor. It was a heroic feat of engineering prowess by a small group of people committed to a very specific goal. Their motto was "Waste anything but time."

But human affairs are not as pliable to the laws of engineering, or science, as social planners would like. We know this from the stack of corpses that crowds out the sun over the twentieth century. Even here where the totalitarian temptation has been kept relatively at bay, we are constantly told that disagreements over facts are indictments over motives. If I tell a liberal that Head Start doesn't work, they skip the data and go straight to saying I am a mean person. A hater.

But as Emerson said, "There is always a certain meanness in the argument of conservatism, joined with a certain superiority in its fact."

Sidney Milkis

The Political Effects of the Great Society

Lyndon Johnson's Great Society, and its legacy for politics and government in the United States, is very hard to grasp. There was something extraordinary about LBJ and his leadership. If his presidency
did not involve the grand politics best displayed by Abraham Lincoln
and Franklin Roosevelt, and that Marc Landy and I associate with
"refoundings," he did play a critical part in bringing about profound
changes in American politics and government. In part, Johnson and
his political allies greatly embellished the New Deal order—and its
dedication to economic security. As one columnist wrote in 1965, the
Johnson administration's initiatives in health care, education, and civil
rights did much to "codify the New Deal vision of the good society."[1]
We surely could debate the merits of these measures that expanded the
New Deal—Medicare, Medicaid, Aid to Elementary and Secondary
Education, and the 1964 and 1965 Civil Rights Acts. But, on the whole,
these programs have been honored by Democrats and Republicans
alike, and have received strong support from what Arthur Schlesinger,
Jr., called the "vital center" of the country.

And yet, at the same time that it embellished the New Deal state,
the Johnson administration helped to initiate an assault on it. The Great

Society encouraged, and helped to legitimize, a new form of liberalism, or a post-modernity, that led to a full-scale assault—not only from the right, but also (mainly) from the left—on "the working arrangements of the entrenched liberal administrative state and society."[2] At the center of that state stood the modern presidency. The national reform fostered by the New Deal shifted the focus of power away from the localized traditional party apparatus, as well as from the more decentralizing institutions—Congress and the state governments. With Roosevelt's long rein, a politics of administration emerged, centered in the White House Office (the West Wing!) and the Executive Office of the presidency, that depended primarily on a presidency-generated administrative state for coherence and energy.

The development of a modern executive that was insulated from parties and local self-government was particularly likely to happen when domestic programs or benefits were defended as rights—and international obligations were viewed as central to the security of individual men and women. The commitment of Roosevelt and his New Deal political allies to uphold two new freedoms—Freedom from Want (welfare state) and Freedom from Fear (national security state)—to "supplement" traditional ones like speech and religion—reinforced centralized administration. Pronounced in Roosevelt's famous Four Freedoms Address (1941), these new rights exalted national administrative power into a new creed—New Deal Liberalism (in a *de facto* sense a second Declaration of Independence)—that demanded the transcendence rather than the transformation of partisanship. FDR's genius was to change American politics without seeming to do so: rights-based centralized state, an "administrative constitution." Dwight Eisenhower, the first GOP president since the Roosevelt "Revolution," bestowed bipartisan legitimacy on this new constitutional order.

The executive-centered administrative state reached its apogee during the Kennedy and Johnson administrations. Addressing a White House news conference in May 1962, Kennedy said:

> Most of us are conditioned for many years to have a political viewpoint—Republican or Democratic—liberal, conservative, moderate. The fact of the matter is that most of the problems [we face today], or at least many of them, are administrative

Society. LBJ and his aides believed that the social movements of the 1960s revealed that America was ready for another, bolder episode of reform. To them, the civil rights revolution demonstrated not only the power and possibility of organized protest, but also the unsuspected fragility of resistance in America to liberating changes. Indeed, the civil rights movement established the model for other social movements that grew out of the 1960s—the feminist movement, consumerism, and environmentalism. Another social movement, the anti-war movement, which literally sprang from the civil rights movement, would help drive LBJ from office. But in the relatively calm early days of LBJ's leadership, aides such as Goodwin, and Johnson himself, envisioned such new social forces as potential agents of a new generation of reform.

In the end, of course, Johnson would become the target, rather than the leader, of these new social forces, a failing often attributed to his ineffective leadership style: Johnson was neither charismatic nor effective at the art of media communication. Unlike Bobby Kennedy, who as one White House aide put it, launched a "war of liberation" against the administration in 1968, Johnson could not succeed at "the politics of existentialism." But LBJ's failure went deeper than inadequate charisma. In the final analysis, it was a failure to understand fully the inherent tension between executive leadership, indeed, the very notion of statesmanship, and the Great Society. The Roosevelt revolution dedicated itself to tangible government entitlements, thereby forging a coalition of African-Americans, labor union members, and white ethnic groups who looked to the modern presidency and the "liberal establishment" for leadership and programmatic benefits. The Great Society extended the reach of government to the "quality" of American lives—consumer and environmental protection, aid to the arts and humanities, and community-based experiments in fighting poverty and racism—that helped to bring to power issue-oriented independents, representing broad causes and movements, who resisted "presidential management"—and were less willing to delegate policy responsibility to administrative agencies. The reformers who took control of the Democratic Party after the 1968 Chicago convention— the so-called McGovern Democrats (supporters of 1972 presidential candidate George McGovern)—followed the New Deal tradition of scorning partisanship. But as my colleague James Ceaser has noted, they rejected the concept of presidential leadership and the practice of centralized administration that had prevailed during the New Deal era. The presidency had to become the *instrument* rather than the *steward* of reform causes and groups.

Most of all, of course, these new liberals rejected strong leadership in foreign policy. Contemporary admirers of Johnson and the Great Society are likely to draw a sharp line between the Great Society and the War in Vietnam, treating Vietnam as a virtual lapse of judgment, an intrusion on Johnson's domestic agenda. But for Johnson and some of his more hawkish aides, there were strong even organic links between the two. A Great Society, they believed, had the duty to exercise the righteous use of force abroad. And yet, the "new liberals" that LBJ sought to ally himself with, those who celebrated liberation and rejected the possibility of *statesmanship*, were, as *The Village Voice* editorialized in 1967, more interested in sympathizing with the unborn revolutions in the Third World, than in [containing Communism] or [strengthening] NATO."

In truth, the Great Society had begun to unravel before the Vietnam War wreaked havoc on the Johnson presidency. It was the domestic War on Poverty, the signature Great Society program, that first exposed the vulnerabilities of "qualitative liberalism." It held that poverty had deep cultural roots; that powerlessness and the absence of community (alienation) afflicted the nation's poor, especially poor African-Americans, living in urban ghettos. As LBJ put it in his famous address at Howard University in 1965, "deep, corrosive, obstinate differences" distinguished black from white poverty—differences that "radiat[ed] painful roots into the [black] community, and into the [black] family, and the nature of the [black] individual." This was not merely rhetorical flourish: The White House task force charged with developing a blueprint for a War on Poverty recommended that community action be made an integral part of it. As a result, policy was delegated to Community Action Program, famously governed by federal guidelines requiring "maximum feasible participation of residents of the areas and groups served."

As Daniel Patrick Moynihan pointed out in his classic 1970 critique of the War on Poverty, *Maximum Feasible Misunderstanding*, the communal concerns of the Johnson presidency were more the result of top-down, rather than bottom-up, reform. The Community Action Program did not respond to the pressure groups of the poor (there were none). They were an administrative invention, Moynihan argued, merely an extension of the modern presidency that did great harm to the remnants of local self-government in the United States. Viewing the states and localities, and the entrenched, usually Democratic, political machines that controlled them as obstacles to the "enlightened" management of social policy, Johnson and his aides expected CAPs to carry out policy conceived in Washington, to serve the Office of Economic Opportunity, headed by Sargent Shriver, which was established in the White House Office as the principal federal poverty agency. Not surprisingly, many grassroots activists felt they were victimized, not empowered, by a program that often seemed overwhelmed by its own complexity and bureaucracy.

Nonetheless, although administrative centralization enervated the participatory aspirations of the War on Poverty, the Johnson administration's rhetoric and policies gave rise to insurgent forces that could not be controlled, indeed took on a life of their own. CAPs eventually proved uncontrollable because they fed into, and gave institutional support to the growing militancy of the civil rights movement, which by 1966 had become deeply dissatisfied with the accomplishments of the Johnson administration. Contrary to what a lot of historians tell us, Johnson did not repudiate these government-subsidized radicals. As I have learned from rooting around Great Society archives, rather than sound a full retreat in the face of this challenge, Johnson sent a number of younger White House aides on an information-gathering mission to various cities to meet with black leaders during the long hot summers of 1966 and 1967, when urban riots swept across the nation. Their lengthy report makes for fascinating testimony of the Johnson administration's dilemma. Above all, they sought to reassure Johnson that even as government-subsidized activists turned on the White House, the Great Society's approach to the politics of race and poverty—emphasizing the political disease of alienation—was working. As Sherwin Markman, who organized the White House ghetto visits, concluded dramatically after spending time in the East Bay communities of Oakland, Berkeley, and Richmond, California, "the only way the Negro can identify with the national government is by being an integral part of it. The War on Poverty is the great bulwark against the total disaffection of the ghetto Negro, which in the long run can only lead to guerilla warfare. The Poverty program succeeds by involving the Negro totally in the dreams and destiny of this nation."[5]

These reports apparently played a pivotal role in persuading Johnson to respond to the riots not with recrimination, but, rather, with redoubled efforts to expand civil rights (1968 Civil Rights bill, Open-Housing). Moreover, Johnson continued to support the War on Poverty in the face of urban riots—persuading Congress to reauthorize this core Great Society program in 1967—even though its Community Action Program was reportedly having a disruptive influence in many cities, and were the target of bitter complaints from local party leaders. The president did not ignore the complaints of local politicians about the CAPS. He feared, during especially dark moments, that they were unduly influenced by "Kooks and Sociologists."[6] Still, encouraged by his staff's ghetto reports, Johnson stuck with the War on Poverty. Having staked his political fortunes in the social movements that it empowered, Johnson had little choice but to support the Office of Economic Opportunity and the community organizations it spawned, even as he grew increasingly aware of the fact that it aroused leadership and social forces that had come to view him "as part of the white apparatus which created and fostered the perpetuation" of racial injustice.[7] He had learned from reading Tocqueville, he told a young aide during a rare reflective moment toward the end of his presidency, that leaders of revolutions often become their victims.

Combining presidential government and "participatory democracy," Johnson intended to build a new liberal coalition dedicated to the cause of blacks, consumers, environmentalists, and women. More penetratingly, in an admittedly halting way, Johnson was seeking to reconcile the New Deal state with the historical American antipathy to the bureaucracy. Instead he became an agent of reform that brought forth a crisis of the liberal order. The two most significant facts of the reforms of the Great Society were the aggrandizement of executive power and, in seeming contrast to that, a deep suspicion of centralized administration. The Community Action Program, resulting from a complex melding of administrative invention and the rejection of centralized administration, perfectly captured the paradox of Lyndon Johnson's Great Society. This intriguing and disconcerting paradox—the Ibsenesque love–hate relationship with administrative power—would intensify during the 1970s. Then liberal advocacy groups, the self-styled public interest organizations that evolved (metastasized) from the social movements of the 1960s, formed an institutional partnership with the courts that both expanded federal commitments—to controversial policies like affirmative action, and further undermined public authority ("participatory democracy" to "citizen suit"). Moreover, as Hugh Heclo has argued, many of the lineal descendants of this odd amalgam of aspiration and alienation in public affairs play large in contemporary American politics. Teaching Americans both to expect more from the government and to trust it less, the Great Society was the fulcrum on which the decline of liberalism and the rise of conservatism tilted. But the rise of a strong conservative movement that would achieve considerable influence by the end of the 1970s and seize power with the elevation of Ronald Reagan to the White House did not completely dispel Great Society civics. Indeed, the Great Society changed not only liberalism but conservatism as well. Rather than dismantling "big government," conservatives dedicated themselves to supporting parallel advocacy groups and think tanks that would deploy national administration and remake the courts in the service of conservative objectives. Consequently, even as they profess a hatred of big government, conservatives have expected it to promote democracy abroad, nurture family values, and hold public schools accountable so that "no child is left behind."

By the dawn of the twenty-first century, Democrats and Republicans, conservatives and liberals, had all become, as Heclo put it, "policy minded." But rather than pursue solutions to the nation's problems with New Deal-style executive-centered and pragmatic policy solutions, contemporary liberal and conservative activists engage in ideological confrontation and institutional combat that defy consensus and diminish public trust in government. This is the conundrum that the Great Society has left us: The challenge to the younger generations is to rediscover American Democracy so that we can escape from the pathological contradictions that affect it.

Notes

1. Richard A. Rovere, "A Man for This Age Too," *New York Times Magazine* (April 11, 1965): 118.
2. Hugh Heclo, "The Sixties False Dawn: Awakenings, Movements, and Postmodern Policy-Making," *Journal of Policy History* 8(1): 41.
3. George Reedy, *The Twilight of the Presidency* (New York: New American Library, 1970), XV.
4. Harry McPherson, interview with the author, Washington, DC, July 30, 1985.
5. Memorandum, Sherwin Markman to the President, March 14, 1967. White House Central Files, We9, Lyndon Baines Johnson Library, Austin, Texas.
6. David Welborn and Jesse Burkhead, *Intergovernmental Relations in the Administrative State* (Austin, TX: University of Texas Press, 1989), 56–76.
7. Memorandum, Sherwin Markman to the President, April 6, 1967. White House Central File, We9, Lyndon Baines Johnson Library, Austin, Texas.

John C. Goodman

Extending the Great Society: Grading the 2010 Health Care Act

Repeal and Replace: Ten Necessary Changes

There are ten structural flaws in the Affordable Care Act (ACA). Each is so potentially damaging, Congress will have to resort to major corrective action even if the critics of the ACA are not involved. Further, each must be addressed in any new attempt to create workable health care reform.

1. An Impossible Mandate

Problem: The ACA requires individuals to buy a health insurance plan whose cost will grow at twice the rate of growth of their incomes. Not only will health care claim more and more of every family's disposable income, the act takes away many of the tools the private sector now uses to control costs.

Solution: (1) Repeal the individual and employer mandates, (2) offer a generous tax subsidy to people to obtain insurance, but (3) allow them the freedom and flexibility to adjust their benefits and cost-sharing in order to control costs.

2. A Bizarre System of Subsidies

Problem: The ACA offers radically different subsidies to people at the same income level, depending on where they obtain their health insurance—at work, through an exchange, or through Medicaid. The subsidies (and the accompanying mandates) will cause millions of employees to lose their employer plans and may cause them to lose their jobs as well. At a minimum, these subsidies will cause a huge, uneconomical restructuring of American industry.

Solution: Offer people the same tax relief for health insurance, regardless of where it is obtained or purchased—preferably in the form of a lump-sum, refundable tax credit.

3. Perverse Incentives for Insurers

Problem: The ACA creates perverse incentives for insurers and employers (worse than under the current system) to attract the healthy and avoid the sick, and to overprovide to the healthy (to encourage them to stay) and underprovide to the sick (to encourage them to leave).

Solution: Instead of requiring insurers to ignore the fact that some people are sicker and more costly to insure than others, adopt a system that compensates them for the higher expected costs—ideally making a high-cost enrollee just as attractive to an insurer as low-cost enrollee.

4. Perverse Incentives for Individuals

Problem: The ACA allows individuals to remain uninsured while they are healthy (paying a small fine or no fine at all) and to enroll in a health plan after they get sick (paying the same premium everyone else is paying). No insurance pool can survive the gaming of the system that is likely to ensue.

Solution: People who remain continuously insured should not be penalized if they have to change insurers; but people who are willfully uninsured should not be able to completely free ride on others by gaming the system.

5. Impossible Expectations/A Tattered Safety Net

Problem: The ACA aims to insure as many as 34 million uninsured people. Economic studies suggest they will try to double their consumption of medical care. Yet the act creates not one new doctor, nurse, or paramedical personnel. We can expect as many as 900,000 additional emergency room visits every year—mainly by new enrollees in Medicaid—and 23 million are expected to remain uninsured. Yet, as was the case in Massachusetts, not only is there no mechanism to ensure that funding will be there for safety net institutions that will shoulder the biggest burdens, their "disproportionate share" funds are slated to be cut.

Solution: (1) Liberate the supply side of the market by allowing nurses, paramedics, and pharmacists to deliver care they are competent to deliver. (2) Allow Medicare and Medicaid to cover walk-in clinics at shopping malls and other unconventional care—paying market prices. (3) Free doctors to provide lower-cost, higher-quality services in the manner described below. And (4) redirect unclaimed health insurance tax credits (for people who elect to remain uninsured) to the safety net institutions in the areas where they live—to provide a source of funds in case they cannot pay their own medical bills.

6. Impossible Benefit Cuts for Seniors

Problem: The ACA's cuts in Medicare are draconian. By 2017, seniors in such cities as Dallas, Houston, and San Antonio will lose one-third of their benefits. By 2020, Medicare nationwide will pay doctors and hospitals less than what Medicaid pays. Seniors will be lined up behind Medicaid patients at community health centers and safety net hospitals unless this is changed. Either these cuts were never a serious way to fund the ACA, because Congress will cave and restore them, or the elderly and the disabled will be in a separate (and inferior) health care system.

Solution: Many of the cuts to Medicare will have to be restored. However, Medicare cost increases can be slowed by empowering patients and doctors to find efficiencies and eliminate waste in the manner described below.

7. Impossible Burden for the States

Problem: Even as the ACA requires people to obtain insurance and fines them if they do not, the states will receive no additional help if the estimated 10 million currently Medicaid-eligible people decide to enroll. Although there is substantial help for the newly eligible enrollees, the states will still face a multibillion dollar, unfunded liability the states cannot afford.

Solution: States need the opportunity and flexibility to manage their own health programs—without federal interference. Ideally, they should receive a block grant with each state's proportion determined by its percent of the nation's poverty population.

8. Lack of Portability

Problem: The single biggest health insurance problem for most Americans is the lack of portability. If history is a guide, 80 percent of the 78 million baby boomers will retire before they become eligible for Medicare. Two-thirds of them have no promise of post-retirement health care from an employer. If they have above-average incomes, they will receive little or no tax relief when they try to purchase insurance in the newly created health insurance exchange. To make matters worse, the ACA appears to encourage employers to drop the post-retirement health plans that are now in place.

Solution: (1) Allow employers to do something they are now barred from doing: purchase personally owned, portable health insurance for their employees. Such insurance should travel with the individual—from job to job and in and out of the labor market. (2) Give retirees the same tax relief now available only to employees. And (3) allow employers and employees to save for post-retirement care in tax-free accounts.

9. Over-Regulated Patients

Problem: The ACA forces people to spend their premium dollars on first-dollar coverage for a long list of diagnostic tests. Yet if everyone in America takes advantage of all of the free preventative care the ACA promises, family doctors will be spending all their time delivering care to basically healthy people—with no time to do anything else. At the same time, the ACA encourages the healthy to over-consume care, it leaves chronic patients trapped in a third-party payment system that is fragmented, uncoordinated, wasteful and, designed for everyone other than the patient.

Solution: (1) Instead of dictating deductibles and copayments, give patients greater freedom to save for their own small dollar expenses in health savings accounts, which they own and control; and let them make their own consumption decisions. (2) Allow the chronically ill access to special health accounts, following the example of Medicaid's highly successful Cash and Counseling program, which allows home-bound, low-income disabled patients to control their own budgets and hire and fire those who provide them with services.

10. Over-Regulated Doctors

Problem: The people in the best position to find ways to reduce costs and increase quality are the nation's 778,000 doctors. Yet today they are trapped in a payment system virtually dictated by Medicare. The ACA promises to make this problem worse by encouraging even more unhealthy government intervention into the practice of medicine.

Solution: Providers should be free to repackage and reprice their services under Medicare. As long as their proposals reduce costs and raise quality, Medicare should encourage resourceful, innovative attempts to create a better health care system.

ROBERT HIGGS

The Economics of the Great Society:
Theories, Policies, and Consequences

The rapid growth of government and the surge of federal economic interventions that occurred during Lyndon B. Johnson's presidency—the much-ballyhooed Great Society, whose centerpiece was the War on Poverty—differed from the four preceding surges in twentieth-century U.S. history, each of which had been sparked by war or economic depression. No national emergency prevailed when Johnson took office following John F. Kennedy's assassination on November 22, 1963. The nation was not engaged in a major shooting war, and the economy was on the mend after the mild recession of 1960–61. According to historian Paul K. Conkin, the Johnson administration "moved beyond a response to pressing constituency pressures, beyond crisis-induced legislative action, to a studied, carefully calculated effort to identify problems and to create the needed constituencies to help solve them." For the most part, the Great Society represented simply the culmination of economic, political, and intellectual developments, revulsions against the free market, and reformist aspirations stretching back as far as the nineteenth century.

After the Korean War armistice of July 27, 1953, the United States had enjoyed a decade of respite from the rapid growth of government power over economic affairs. The wartime wage, price, and production

27

controls lapsed, although authority to reinstitute the production controls remained. No major extensions of the government's economic controls were enacted. Big government did not disappear, of course; many of the controls and other interventions put in place in the 1930s and 1940s remained in force. But businessmen, according to economist Herbert Stein, "had learned to live with and accept most of the regulations." Government spending, especially for Social Security benefits, crept upward. All in all, though, the Eisenhower and Kennedy administrations were placid in comparison with their immediate predecessors and successors.

Under Johnson, however, the federal government's intrusion into economic life swelled enormously. In little more than two years after LBJ took office, according to Conkin, "Congress enacted over two hundred major bills and at least a dozen landmark measures.... The ferment, the chaos, rivaled that of 1933, and all at a scope at least four times greater than the early New Deal." Major events included enactment of the Civil Rights Act of 1964, the Economic Opportunity Act of 1964, the Food Stamp Act of 1964, the Elementary and Secondary Education Act of 1965, and the Social Security Amendments of 1965 (creating Medicare and Medicaid), as well as establishment of the Office of Economic Opportunity (to oversee programs such as VISTA, Job Corps, Community Action Program, and Head Start), hundreds of Community Action Agencies, and many other bureaus ostensibly promoting poor people's health, education, job training, and welfare. In addition, during Johnson's presidency, broad-gauge economic regulatory measures were adopted in connection with traffic safety, coal-mine safety, consumer-products safety, age discrimination in employment, truth in lending, and other areas. Conkin concludes: "In five years the American government approximately doubled its regulatory role and at least doubled the scope of transfer payments."

Ideological and Political Context of the Great Society

What accounts for this multifaceted outburst? Do its various elements have a common denominator? Some scholars point to an intellectual development that Stein dubs "Galbraithianism," after its leading propagator John Kenneth Galbraith—a loose collection of socioeconomic analysis and evaluation hostile to the free market and favorably in-clined toward more sweeping government controls. "There was," says Stein, "no demand for a new and different economic system" in the Galbraithian view. Rather, "[t]he ideological case for the old system, the free market, capitalist system, was punctured by the demonstration of exceptions to its general rules and claims, and this opened the way for specific policy interventions and measures of income redistribution without any visible limits."

Galbraithianism's arguments and attitudes gained strength from a spreading conviction that the U.S. economy would continue to grow forever at a fairly high rate, thereby ensuring that new and costly gov-ernment programs could easily be financed by drawing on the so-called "growth dividend."

Economist Henry Aaron's description of the climate of opinion in the 1960s essentially agrees with Stein's. Aaron also traces the widely held Galbraithianism back to previous crises:

> The faith in government action, long embraced by reformers
> and spread to the mass of the population by depression and
> war, achieved political expression in the 1960s. This faith was
> applied to social and economic problems, the perceptions
> of which were determined by simplistic and naïve popular
> attitudes and by crude analyses of social scientists.

As the observations of the conservative Stein and the left-liberal Aaron illustrate, scholars of diverse ideological persuasions agree that prevailing attitudes among both elites and masses in the mid-1960s favored increased government intervention in the market economy. Thus, ideological postures engendered or fostered by past crises had come once again into political prominence. Such public attitudes reached their high tide during 1964 and 1965, the first two full years of Johnson's presidency. Historian John A. Andrew III describes the mid-1960s as "a liberal interlude unmatched in the twentieth century, except perhaps for the mid-1930s."

Although the 1960s are now often recalled as a sort of radical outburst against established American orthodoxies in economic, social, and political affairs, it would be a mistake to suppose that the business class opposed the dominant strains of political thought and action at that time. Businessmen, observed *Time* magazine in December 1965, "have come to accept that the Government should actively use its Keynesian tools to promote growth and stability." Thus, when LBJ stood for election in 1964, as historian Allen J. Matusow has written, "the sweetest returns of all came from Wall Street":

> The nation's corporate elite, abandoning its traditional preference for the GOP, voted for the party that had stimulated sales, fueled profits, and lowered corporate taxes. An estimated 60 percent or more of the Business Council—the semi-official link between the corporations and the government—favored LBJ. The lion's share of the big contributions flowed into his campaign coffers. And on September 3 [1964] a group of corporate leaders met in the White House to organize a business committee for Johnson's re-election. Its forty-five founding members included Henry Ford II, Edgar Kaiser of Kaiser Aluminum, Joseph Block of Inland Steel, two members of Eisenhower's Cabinet, and several New York bankers. Corporate liberalism paid big dividends for the Democrats at last.

When given a choice between free-market ideology and crony-capitalist proceeds, the leaders of big business tended to follow the money.

Moreover, in those days, a so-called New Class—composed of scientists, lawyers and judges, city planners, social workers, professors, criminologists, public health doctors, reporters, editors, and commentators in the news media, among others—viewed new government programs as outlets for their "idealism" and as opportunities to do well while doing good. Thus, a multitude of left-leaning intellectuals and pseudo-intellectuals gave significant leadership, support, and voice to the government's surge during the Johnson years.

More prosaic political developments also played an important role. Lyndon Johnson, who began his career as a New Dealer and political horse-trader in Texas, possessed not only boundless energy and ambition, but also keen political instincts and skills; he knew how to move Congress in the direction he wanted it to go. Moreover, the 1964 elections gave the Democrats huge majorities in both houses of Congress and brought into office an extraordinarily leftish group of freshman legislators. According

to Aaron, "No administration since Franklin Roosevelt's first had operated subject to fewer political constraints than President Johnson's."

The specific forms the Great Society took reflected the increasing
diversity of animals in the political jungle. While longstanding lobbies
for business, labor unions, farmers, and middle-class professional groups
continued to operate, many new interest groups organized and gained
political clout on behalf of so-called "oppressed minorities": women,
Indians, Chicanos, students, homosexuals, the handicapped, the elderly,
and many others, none of whom had been directly represented as such
to an important extent in U.S. politics. These groups demanded that the
federal government solve a variety of racial, urban, employment, and
consumer problems, real and imagined. As Conkin notes,

> Each of [the] Great Society commitments promised benefits
> to a targeted and often an increasingly self-conscious interest
> group (blacks, the aged, the educationally deprived, the poor,
> the unemployed, urban ghetto dwellers, consumers, nature
> enthusiasts). In no case did the targeted recipients of new favors
> have either the political clout or the leadership to gain the leg-
> islation. But in each case their visibility or their protest helped
> create broader attention and concern. Passage of each major
> Great Society bill thus depended upon a broad coalition.

Galbraithianism, Marxism, New Leftism, and other varieties of
critical socioeconomic analysis also helped to justify the displacement
of anti-war and pro-civil-rights enthusiasms onto a diverse set of anti-
market causes, giving rise to heightened support for environmental,
consumer, and zero-risk regulations. No perceived social or economic
problem seemed out of bounds in this cacophonous new political
environment. Faith in the government's ability to solve social and economic problems reached a new high. Regardless of the nature of the
problem—racial antipathy, unemployment, illiteracy, poor nutrition,
inadequate housing, workplace accidents, insufficient cultivation of
the arts, unsightly roadsides, environmental pollution, and a thousand
other real and perceived problems, spanning the full range of social
and economic life—both intellectual elites and the mass public agreed
in large part that the solution took the same general form: The federal
government should "do something" or, if the government were already

engaged, it should act more vigorously or on a larger scale. In particular, in one way or another, it should spend more money.

Nevertheless, although the Great Society established critically important new federal powers and agencies, it did not cause total federal domestic spending to increase tremendously at first. A portentous sign might have been seen, however, in the quick acceleration of federal transfer payments, which increased from $34.2 billion in 1963 to $65.5 billion in 1969. Over time, this fiscal locomotive gained more and more momentum. Thus, according to Michael D. Tanner, between 1963 and 2010, "the federal government spent more than $13 trillion fighting poverty."

Almost everyone now acknowledges that federal entitlement programs, crowned by the enormously costly health-care systems the Great Society spawned, have promised much greater benefits than the government can fund indefinitely, and hence many of these benefits will have to be cut, notwithstanding the political fury such cuts surely will elicit. This impending sociopolitical tumult represents one of the Great Society's bitterest fruits.

Economic Analysis and Great Society Programs

Although the Great Society should be understood as primarily a political phenomenon—a vast conglomeration of government policies and actions based on, expressive of, and responsive to political stances and objectives—economists and economic analysis played important supporting roles in the overall drama. Even when political actors could not have cared less about economic analysis, they were usually at pains to cloak their proposals in some sort of economic rationale. If much of this rhetoric now seems to be little more than shabby window dressing, we might well remind ourselves that the situation in this regard is no better now than it was then—witness, for example, the stampede of mainstream economists back to vulgar Keynesian remedies in wake of the economic crisis that assumed panic proportions in 2008.

Regardless of how political actors in the 1960s might have sought to exploit economic analysis to gain a plausible public-interest rationale for their proposed programs, the most prominent body of economic analysis in those days—the sort taught by the leading lights at Harvard,

Yale, Berkeley, and most of the other great universities—virtually cried out to be exploited in this way. During the mid-1960s—as luck would have it, the very years during which I was learning economics in four different colleges and universities—the so-called Neoclassical Synthesis (a term coined by Paul Samuelson) achieved its greatest hold on the economics profession. By "synthesis," this term refers to the combination of a microeconomic part, which contains the theory of individual markets that had been developed over the preceding two centuries, and a macroeconomic part, which contains the ideas about national economic aggregates advanced in John Maynard Keynes's landmark 1936 book *The General Theory of Employment, Interest and Money* as further developed, systematized, and extended by (some of) Keynes's followers during the three decades after the book's publication. (Note that not all leading economists accepted the Neoclassical Synthesis as an accurate representation of Keynes's own views. Joan Robinson, for example, called it "bastard Keynesianism.")

On the microeconomic side, the Neoclassical Synthesis incorporated the so-called New Welfare Economics that had been developed during the 1930s, 1940s, and 1950s. In this form, microeconomic theory advanced a general equilibrium theory of the economy's various markets, identified the conditions for the attainment of equilibrium in this idealized system, and demonstrated that various "problems"—springing from external effects, collective goods, less-than-perfect information, and less-than-perfect competition, among other conditions—would cause the system to settle in a state of overall inefficiency, causing the value of total output to fall short of the maximum that would have resulted from systemic efficiency, given the economy's available resources of labor and capital and its existing technology. Attainment of such an inefficient state was characterized as a "market failure," and economists expended enormous efforts in alleging the existence of such market failures in real-world markets and in proposing means (e.g., taxes, subsidies, regulations) by which the government might, in theory, at least, remedy these failures and thus maximize "social welfare."

Had economic theorists rested content with using the microeconomics of the Neoclassical Synthesis strictly as a conceptual device employed in abstract reasoning, it might have done little damage. However, as I have already suggested, this type of theory cried out for application—which, in practice, was nearly always *mis*application. The idealized conditions required for theoretical general-equilibrium efficiency could not possibly obtain in the real world; yet the economists readily endorsed government measures aimed at coercively pounding the real world into conformity with these impossible theoretical conditions. Closely examined, such efforts represented a form of madness. Moreover, as the great economist James Buchanan observes, the economists' obsession with general equilibrium gives rise to "the most sophisticated fallacy in [neoclassical] economic theory, the notion that because certain relationships hold in equilibrium the forced interferences designed to implement these relationships will, in fact, be desirable."

Great Society measures such as the Elementary and Secondary Education Act (1965), the Higher Education Act (1965), the Motor Vehicle Safety Act (1966), and the Truth in Lending Act (1968), as well as many of the consumer-protection and environmental-protection laws and regulations, found ready endorsement among contemporary neoclassical economists, who viewed them as proper means for the correction of imagined market failures.

The assumptions that underlay these economic interpretations and applications, however, could be sustained only by wishful thinking. Economists presumed to know where general equilibrium lay, or at least to know the direction in which various inputs and outputs should be changed in order to approach general-equilibrium efficiency more closely. But neoclassical economists cannot move the earth with a mathematical lever, because they have no place to stand—no "given" information about (presumably fixed) property rights, consumer preferences, resource availabilities, and technical possibilities. What neoclassical economics takes as given is, in reality, revealed only by competitive processes. "Most modern economists," Buchanan aptly concludes, "are simply doing what other economists are doing while living off a form of dole that will simply not stand critical scrutiny." Yet, critics such as Buchanan were hardly numerous during the 1960s. In my own training in economics, between 1962 and 1968, I encountered only one of them—Buchanan himself, when he made a seminar presentation at Johns Hopkins while I was a graduate student there. In this regard, my education was typical of what other students were being taught during those years.

If the microeconomic side of the Neoclassical Synthesis fostered government measures to remedy a variety of putative market failures, its macroeconomic side endorsed government measures to remedy the greatest alleged market failure of all—the economy's overall instability and its frequent failure to bring about a condition known as "full employment." The supposition that mass unemployment constituted or reflected a market failure came easily to young economists who had come of age during the Great Depression. In those years of seemingly endless subpar economic performance, all sorts of ideas had been advanced to explain what was wrong and what should be done to repair the economy. Keynes's ideas had many competitors, most of them utterly crackpot. The longstanding commitment of economists to Classical Economics did not collapse completely during the 1930s, but it came under increasing strain, and many good economists who should have known better—men such as Henry Simons, Aaron Director, and Frank Knight—capitulated to unsound, but increasingly influential ideas. In the 1940s, however, the dam burst completely, at least for the elite members of the economics profession, and by the early 1950s, Keynesian ideas had entrenched themselves solidly. Since then, some species of Keynesianism has been either in the professional saddle or clamoring to get there. *Time* magazine observed in December 1965, "Now Keynes and his ideas, though they still make some people nervous, have been so widely accepted that they constitute both the new orthodoxy in the universities and the touchstone of economic management in Washington." Although the stagflation of the 1970s and the rise of the New Classical school seemed for a while to have banished Keynesianism from the leading circles of the economics profession—at least in its form circa the 1960s—vulgar Keynesianism came back with astonishing vigor in the wake of the panic of 2008 and the subsequent recession.

In the mid-1960s, however, these events lay far in the future, and the Neoclassical Synthesis reigned supreme among American economists in the profession's upper reaches. Thus, John F. Kennedy obtained advice about economic policy from Paul Samuelson in 1960 and 1961, and President Johnson maintained a Council of Economic Advisers headed in succession by three prominent Keynesian macroeconomists— Walter Heller, Gardner Ackley, and Arthur M. Okun, and including others, such as Otto Eckstein and James Duesenberry. Thus, whatever advice Johnson received from his council accorded with the tenets of the Neoclassical Synthesis. Among economists outside the Johnson administration, the Neoclassical Synthesis received its most influential exposition from such lions of the economics profession as Samuelson, John R. Hicks, Robert Solow, James Tobin, Lawrence Klein, and Franco Modigliani—all future winners of the Nobel Prize in economics. In its December 31, 1965, issue, *Time* magazine quoted Milton Friedman, whom it described as "the nation's leading conservative economist," as saying: "We are all Keynesians now."

In Classical Economics, long periods of mass unemployment had been regarded as impossible, because such a condition represented a gross, sustained disequilibrium in the labor market, and normal economic changes, especially reductions in the real wage rate, would tend to restore an equilibrium in which the amount of labor services that workers wished to supply equaled the amount that employers wished to demand, and hence no involuntary unemployment of labor would exist. Keynes and his followers insisted, however, that in modern economies, wages and prices were not as flexible as they were assumed to be in Classical Economics. Real wage rates might not fall (or might not fall enough), notwithstanding extraordinarily great unemployment of labor. In this view, the only way to reduce such sustained mass unemployment was by increasing the demand for products, thereby increasing the quantity of labor services employers demanded even at the given, rigid level of real wages.

Further, to bring about such an increase in "aggregate demand"— the overall amount spent for new final goods and services per period of time—reliance on private consumers and investors might prove unavailing. Consumers, whose incomes would be diminished by the lost earnings occasioned by mass unemployment, could play only a passive role. Investors might fail to save the day because of what Keynes's called a lapse of their "animal spirits," which, to be frank, was no explanation at all, but merely a name given to a mysteriously shrunken amount of private demand for new capital goods. In this situation, aggregate demand could be raised sufficiently only from a third source, namely, increased government spending for newly produced goods and services, financed by government borrowing. Moreover, such increased government spending would not only raise aggregate demand directly, but would also have a so-called "multiplier effect," whereby private incomes would be increased, and expenditure of these increased money receipts would set in motion a continuing series of greater demand, increased employment, higher income, and so on, by which the economy might ultimately be pushed to a state of full employment.

In the 1960s, few economists disputed this general framework of analysis. Even critics such as Milton Friedman accepted it, arguing only that certain second-order aspects of the model—for example, the quantitative response of aggregate demand to an increase in the quantity of money—differed from what the Keynesians assumed. In the 1960s, few macroeconomists looked to monetary policy changes as important means of pushing an economy out of what they viewed as a mass-unemployment equilibrium. For the typical macroeconomist of the day, fiscal policy—changes in government spending, taxing, and borrowing—held the key to keeping the economy on a stable growth path. As if to certify the completeness of Keynesianism's conquest, *Time* magazine put an image of Keynes on its December 31, 1965, cover and featured a long, laudatory article titled "We Are All Keynesians Now."

Keynesians recognized that using fiscal policy to alleviate mass unemployment might be overdone, however, raising aggregate demand so high that its main effect became not so much a further increase in employment as an increase in the rate of (overall consumer price) infla-tion. To analyze this problem, they developed what became known as the Phillips Curve, an empirically derived, inverse relationship between the rate of unemployment and the rate of inflation. They also made numerous attempts to estimate the precise parameters of this curve. Above all, they assumed its stability over time. If indeed it was stable, it offered policymakers a menu of choices from which to select: com-binations of the rate of unemployment and the corresponding rate of inflation. If they were willing to tolerate a higher rate of inflation, for example, they could use increases in deficit-financed government spend-ing to push the rate of unemployment down further. Using fiscal policy in this fashion came to be known as "fine tuning" the macroeconomy. Fine tuning was an economic technocrat's dream come true, assuming that it really worked. However, as economist Edmund S. Phelps noted in 1974, "there was absolutely nothing in economic theory that would have lent significant support to such a belief."

President Johnson was fortunate in regard to economic stabilization and growth during his term in office, although he does deserve credit for pushing Kennedy's stalled tax-cut proposal to quick enactment in February 1964. Still, the economy was already growing and the rate of unemployment declining when LBJ took office in November 1963, and macroeconomic conditions continued to improve throughout his presidency, although the rate of inflation began to edge up after 1965, reaching almost 5 percent during his final year. Between 1963 and 1968, real GDP increased by 29 percent, or by 5.2 percent per year on average. The rate of unemployment declined from 5.7 percent in November 1963, when LBJ became president, to 3.4 percent in January 1969, when he left office. This macroeconomic success owed nothing to policymakers' fine tuning, because neither the administration nor the Congress succeeded in making such delicate adjustments of fiscal policy as economic conditions changed. In truth, fine-tuned fiscal policy was impossible in the context of the U.S. government's institutional realities. Even more than Calvin Coolidge, Johnson was simply lucky in the coincidence of his economic policies and the robust performance of the economy.

In any event, this remarkable macroeconomic performance probably deserves the lion's share of the credit for the reduction in measured poverty that occurred during the Great Society years. Of course, the administration proposed, enacted, and implemented a plethora of bills aimed in one way or another at reducing poverty. Indeed, for many observers, the Great Society is virtually synonymous with the War on Poverty. In general, however, nearly all of the anti-poverty measures, to the extent that they met with any success at all, had only a small effect on the national poverty rate, which fell from 19.5 percent in 1963 to 12.8 percent in 1968. Many of the anti-poverty programs had scant funding, and the news coverage they received was out of proportion to the amount of money they received. Some of them, such as the urban renewal programs, were probably counterproductive; most of them were probably neither fish nor fowl, but only more taxpayer money spent with nothing much to show for their display of good intentions. "[T]hose who most directly benefited," says Matusow, "were the middle-class doctors, teachers, social workers, builders, and bankers who provided federally subsidized goods and services of sometimes suspect value."

As Tanner has recently remarked, apropos of the War on Poverty and its programmatic legacies:

> Throwing money at the problem has neither reduced poverty nor made the poor self-sufficient. Instead, government programs have torn at the social fabric of the country and been a significant factor in increasing out-of-wedlock births with all of their attendant problems. They have weakened the work ethic and contributed to rising crime rates. Most tragically of all, the pathologies they engender have been passed on from parent to child, from generation to generation. In fact, the whole theory underlying our welfare programs is wrong-headed. We focus far too much on making poverty more comfortable, and not enough on creating the prosperity that will get people out of poverty.

The Great Society at least did not bring economic growth to a halt, and therefore it did not preclude a continuation of the long-term reduction in the proportion of Americans living in poverty. As for the Johnson administration's War on Poverty in particular, however, no such benign evaluation is justified. Matusow, who can scarcely be described as a spear carrier for conservative dogma, concludes that "the War on Poverty was destined to be one of the great failures of twentieth-century liberalism."

The Great Society programs, whether for macroeconomic fine tuning, microeconomic remedy of alleged market failures, or redistributions of income and wealth to reduce the incidence of poverty had an important element in common: the presumption that technocrats possessed the knowledge and capacity to identify what needed to be done, to design appropriate remedial measures, and to implement those measures successfully. In short, the Great Society amounted to social engineering—or, worse, to sheer, groping, social experimentation—on a grand scale. The planners more or less presumed the existence of private-sector problems and took for granted that they could successfully solve those problems through the use of government's coercive power and the taxpayers' money. They did not give much weight—indeed, they often gave no weight whatsoever—to the possibility of what later came to be known in public choice theory as "government failure." Thus, seeing apparent market failures that left the economy in an inefficient configuration, they supposed that they could identify exactly what to tax, subsidize, or regulate and exactly how much to do so in order to move the economy into an efficient configuration. According to LBJ's biographer Paul Conkin, Johnson "never easily conceded that any except purely private problems did not lend themselves to a political answer. That is, government could directly or indirectly alleviate any distress." As White House aide Joseph Califano later confessed, "We did not recognize that government could not do it all." Yet, to describe the Great Society's multifaceted undertakings as merely hubristic would be too kind to their promoters.

All too many of the programs fell short of even this species of defectiveness, amounting to little more than garden-variety efforts to divert taxpayer money in the service of purely personal and political gain for the insiders who designed, operated, and received benefits from the programs. For example, the Community Action Program, unforget-tably lampooned by Tom Wolfe in his 1970 book *Mau-Mauing the Flak Catchers*, combined ample components of white middle-class guilt, minority shakedowns, and money thrown around basically to appease the menacing claimants who, having been invited to snatch the money, resorted to whatever form of intimidation would get it for them quick-est. "The money," Conkin concludes, "often seemed to dwindle away, funding little more than the wages of [community action agency] employees." More generally, as Andrew notes, "Through 'iron triangles' and the use of clientele capture, the very objects of Great Society reforms all too often seized control of the process to block significant change and enhance their own interests."

Level-headed analysts could scarcely have been shocked by this outcome. As Adam Smith long ago remarked, although the "man of system"—preeminent examples of which played leading roles in initiat-ing the Great Society—treats the members of society as if they were but pieces on a chess board, the people actually have a motive power of their own. In the mid-1960s, the people whom the social and eco-nomic planners undertook to "reform" in various ways refused to sit still while the technocrats treated them as lab rats. Instead, they often reacted by resisting, diverting, or seizing control of the "top-down" plans the government sought to impose on them, causing what, from the planners' perspective, seemed to be program failures. One man's failed experiment, however, was often another man's fulfilled political ambition or bulging bank account. Across the country, for example, local politicians diverted federal money intended to fund Great Society "reform" measures into support for prosaic, local political priorities.

Conclusion

The economics of the Great Society, whether we consider it from the perspective of economic theory, economic policies, or the consequences of those policies, offers much to criticize and little to praise. The theory—the Neoclassical Synthesis—combined a microeconomic theory focused on the identification and rectification of market failures and a macroeconomic theory based on primitive, deeply flawed Keynesianism. Although this body of analysis might sometimes arrive at constructive proposals by accident, as it did when it helped to push through the 1964 tax cut, in general it fostered unconstructive or even counterproductive policies whose common element was increased government intervention in the market system. The best thing we can say for the Great Society economic programs as a whole is that they amounted to a gigantic waste of the taxpayers' money. Many, however, were worse than wastes; they actually caused harm.

Viewed from today's perspective, the Great Society seems to have been above all an almost preposterously bloated collection of social-engineering projects. The mentality that underlay this panoply of policies and actions was one of arrogance and presumption: the presupposition that the leading intellectuals, "the best and the brightest," ought to, and knew how to rearrange the pieces on the human chess board to construct a better society from the top down. Of course, the politicians who joined in this carnival of folly, for the most part, did not care one way or another about intellectual presumptions or positions; they simply saw an inviting opportunity to feather the nests of their supporters, while accruing wealth, public acclaim, and power for themselves. Naturally opportunists of all sorts, from welfare hustlers to subsidy-seeking real estate developers, came running to the fountain from which such copious quantities of the taxpayers' money were flowing.

After 1965, as the civil rights revolution dissolved into urban riots and violent splinter groups and as the growing U.S. engagement in Vietnam lengthened American casualty lists and increased Pentagon outlays, the public first soured and then turned increasingly against both LBJ's domestic program and his foreign war. By 1968, if not earlier, the president had conceded the impossibility of his re-election, and his leading advisers had lost much of their previous enthusiasm for the administration's crusades at home and abroad. Although Richard M. Nixon was elected in 1968, many elements of the Great Society lived on, and some were extended and made ever more expensive, especially the food stamp program, Medicaid, and Medicare. Indeed, the currently looming fiscal train wreck associated with the federal medical-care programs attests that in fundamental ways, the U.S. economy continues to suffer grave damage as a consequence of programs initiated during the Great Society.

Selected References

Aaron, Henry J. 1978. *Politics and the Professors: The Great Society in Perspective.* Washington, DC: Brookings Institution.

Andrew, John A., III. 1998. *Lyndon Johnson and the Great Society.* Chicago: Ivan R. Dee.

Buchanan, James M. 1979. "General Implications of Subjectivism in Economics." In *What Should Economists Do?*, 81–91. Indianapolis, IN: Liberty Fund.

Conkin, Paul K. 1986. *Big Daddy from the Pedernales: Lyndon Baines Johnson.* Boston: Twayne Publishers.

Higgs, Robert. 1987. *Crisis and Leviathan: Critical Episodes in the Growth of American Government.* New York: Oxford University Press.

Matusow, Allen J. 1984. *The Unraveling of America: A History of Liberalism in the 1960s.* New York: Harper and Row.

Phelps, Edmund S. 1974. "Economic Policy and Unemployment in the 1960s." In *The Great Society: Lessons for the Future,* edited by Eli Ginsberg and Robert M. Solow, 30–46. New York: Basic Books.

Stein, Herbert. 1984. *Presidential Economics: The Making of Economic Policy from Roosevelt to Reagon and Beyond.* New York: Simon and Schuster.

Tanner, Michael D. 2010. "More Proof We Can't Stop Poverty by Making It More Comfortable." *Investor's Business Daily,* September 17.

"The Economy: We Are All Keynesians Now," *Time,* December 31, 1965.

CHARLES MURRAY

Losing Ground:
Update on the War on Poverty

I have not changed my analysis of the effects of the Great Society since I published *Losing Ground* in 1984. Therefore, I am not going to give you charts showing what has happened to the poverty rate since the end of the 1960s. I am not going to spend any time on an indictment of the policies of the 1960s. Instead, I want to offer an update on the War on Poverty in a more fundamental way.

The data portions of *Losing Ground* consisted of a set of chapters showing trendlines on things such as poverty, marriage, employment, crime, and education, comparing the white population with the black population. But comparing whites with blacks was a second-best choice. As I pointed out in the introduction to Part II of *Losing Ground*, "What we would really like is a longitudinal sample of the disadvantaged.... If social policy is successful, we should see improvement in their situation over time." But I couldn't produce such trendlines in 1984, the data not being available. The best alternative was to use blacks as the proxy for the longitudinal sample of "disadvantaged Americans" that would have been preferable.

Now, those barriers have been removed. Whereas in 1984, we social scientists had to rely on whatever breakdowns the government chose to publish from the Current Population Survey, today I have all the raw data from the CPS from the 1960s through 2010 sitting on my computer. I have all the raw data from the General Social Survey from 1972 through 2008. I have all of the raw data from all of the National Longitudinal Surveys. And more.

We are freed from the constraint of comparing blacks and whites, and can focus on different socioeconomic classes of Americans. In the book I am working on now, I take an additional step to make the story as clear as possible. I have eliminated all the complications associated with interpreting how minorities have fared. Instead, I focus on a population that has no excuses—no language barrier, no legacy of slavery, no problematic cultural baggage. I update the fortunes of those toward the bottom of American society by focusing exclusively on the statistics for whites of European origin. I not only update the trends for those at the bottom, but look at trends for those at the top as well.

What I am about to present leads me to conclude that the United States since 1960 has developed a new lower class—not the black underclass, but a lower class of whites, growing in size, who are falling away from the virtues and practices that the Founders assumed were necessary for a free society to function. Since 1960 the United States has developed a new upper class, increasingly segregated from, indifferent to, and ignorant of, the rest of America.

As a convenient way to think about these two groups, I use the Current Population Survey and other databases to create two fictional neighborhoods. One is called Belmont and the other is Fishtown. Belmont is named after an affluent suburb of Boston where a dear friend of mine, the late Richard Herrnstein, lived while we co-authored *The Bell Curve*. My fictional Belmont consists of people who are college-educated and work in managerial positions or in a prestigious profession—doctors, attorneys, scientists, college faculty, and the like. Fishtown is named after a neighborhood in Philadelphia that has been a white working-class neighborhood since before the Revolution. In my fictional Fishtown, everybody works in a blue-collar job, a low-level white collar job, or a low-skill service job. Some don't have an occupation at all. Educationally no one in my fictional Fishtown has more than a high school education.

This leaves a lot of people in the middle—highly skilled technicians, nurses, mid-level white collar people, K-12 teachers, police detectives—

who are not represented in the numbers I am about to present. I analyzed their trends as well, and I can tell you how they came out: They are always in the middle.

One other peculiarity about my fictional neighborhoods: I restrict the analysis to people in the prime of their adult lives, ages 30 to 49. That eliminates a lot of other complications associated with changes in the age of marriage among the young and changes in the age of retirement among the old.

I begin with the new lower class and five indicators: marriage, the labor market, crime, religiosity, and social capital.

Marriage. In 1960, when the story begins, just about all adults in their 30s and 40s were married, in Fishtown and Belmont alike. Then, starting around 1970, marriage took a nosedive that lasted for nearly twenty years for the nation as a whole. But it didn't happen equally to both neighborhoods. By the mid-1980s, the decline in marriage had stopped in Belmont. Marriage rates in Fishtown kept falling.

The net result is that the two neighborhoods, which had been only 11 percentage points apart as late as 1978 in the percentage of persons who were married, were separated by 35 percentage points as of 2010, when only a minority of prime-age whites in Fishtown were married: 48 percent in 2010, compared to 84 percent in 1960.

Some of the change in Fishtown was caused by the rise in divorce, which was much higher in Fishtown than in Belmont. But much of it is attributed to the fact that increasing numbers of people in Fishtown never got married in the first place, especially males. As of 2010, almost one out of three Fishtown males ages 30 to 49 had not yet married. That is a troubling percentage.

An even more troubling percentage has to do with family formation. Over the last two decades, all scholars who are familiar with the data—liberal as well as conservative scholars—have concluded that family structure is hugely important for the development of children. No matter what the outcome being examined—school dropout rate, emotional health, unemployment as adults, substance abuse, educational attainment, or any other measure of how well or poorly children do in life—on average, the family structure that produces the best outcomes for children are two biological parents who remain married. Divorced parents produce the next-best outcomes. Never-married women produce the worst outcomes. All of these statements apply after controlling for the family's socioeconomic status.

With that in mind, consider births to unmarried women in Belmont and Fishtown. In Belmont, they are still at 1950 levels—around 6 percent of all births. In Fishtown—consisting exclusively of non-Hispanic whites, remember—about 45 percent of all births occur to unmarried women. This is going to be as catastrophic for Fishtown as it has been for the black inner city.

Let's turn to the world of work. In 1960, almost all white males in the prime of life were either working fulltime or trying to work fulltime, and that was true in Fishtown as well as Belmont. In 2008, *before* the recession started, about 14 percent of Fishtown men were not even in the labor force. Unemployment among Fishtown men who were in the labor force was higher than the national unemployment rate would lead one to predict. Twenty percent of Fishtown men with jobs were working fewer than 40 hours a week, even when jobs were plentiful.

What about crime? Everybody knows that the crime rate soared in the 1960s and 1970s, but the good news is that both violent and property crime have declined substantially since the early 1990s—by about 40 percent. But that national picture is almost irrelevant to thinking about your safety. If you live in Belmont, the national increase in crime never made much difference in your life. Affluent, suburban America has never experienced much of a rise in crime. Had you lived in Fishtown, you would have watched crime skyrocket from 1960 through the 1980s. Things have improved only marginally since then. In addition to that, the percentage of Fishtown males who are now in prison has quadrupled.

Religion. One of the fascinating things about the founding of the United States is that although almost all the Founders were less than orthodox in their religious beliefs, they were all emphatic about the role of religion as a crucial force in making a free society possible. All of them believed that when the state does not coerce behavior, humans must be self-governing—restraining their own behavior voluntarily—and that religious belief fostered that self-restraint. Speaking as a social scientist, I am convinced there is a lot of contemporary evidence that they were right. In that context, here is a finding that you may find surprising: America has become much more secular across the board than it was in

1960, but Fishtown has become much more secular than Belmont. More than half of adults in Fishtown are not engaged in religion at all. Among those who are, fewer than half attend worship services regularly.

The implications of this go beyond issues of self-governance, which brings us to the final measure for documenting the new lower class—social capital. "Social capital" refers to all the social and civic activities that have created vibrant American communities that could solve their own problems. As Robert Putnam documented in his best-seller, *Bowling Alone*, social capital in America has plummeted since 1960. Furthermore, he found that about half of all the social capital in America's communities is religion-related. Given what has happened to religion in Fishtown, it is not surprising to learn that social capital in Fishtown has also collapsed. But apart from the religious aspect, membership in civic organizations has fallen, membership in social organizations has fallen, and voting and other forms of political participation has fallen. To top it off, social trust has gone through the floor. According to the General Social Survey of 2008, only about 20 percent of Fishtown people responded positively to the question, "Generally speaking, would you say that most people can be trusted or that you can't be too careful in dealing with people?" When 80 percent of the people don't trust their neighbors, social capital cannot thrive.

The common theme for all of these indicators is straightforward. In 1960, white America really did have a common culture in which very large majorities of people participated, whether they were poor or rich, poorly educated or highly educated. As of now, white America has diverged on some of the most fundamental demographic measures. There are still plenty of Americans in Fishtown who are doing their best—but increasingly they live in communities that have large minorities of their populations who are not doing their best, and who are making life difficult for everyone else. We have a new lower class that has sprung up since the 1960s and that has nothing to do with race, with illegal immigration, or any other kind of problems associated with our nation's ethnic diversity. We have dry rot among the whites of European origin who have always been the dominant component of the American population.

Some may infer some good news in this otherwise dreary recital of trends—that Belmont seems to be doing pretty well. Although working-class America has developed some serious problems, at least the people toward the top are still getting married, working hard, not committing crimes, and, at least to some degree, are still engaged in their religions. That's good news, right?

The answer is yes if we take Belmont as a whole. If we look at the most successful layer of Belmont, however, a new set of issues arise, associated with what I will call the new upper class. To illustrate what I mean, let me tell you a tale of three cities—Austin, Texas; Manhattan; and Newton, Iowa.

When the 1960 census was taken, Austin was still a small city with a population of just 187,000. It was the state capital and home to the University of Texas, but otherwise Austin was mainly a center for receiving and shipping agricultural products from the surrounding farm country. Some local companies manufactured brick, tile, and bedroom furniture—that was about it.

The rich people of Austin lived to the west of downtown. But "rich" wasn't all that rich. The median family income in the four richest census tracts was just $60,000. That's $60,000 in today's dollars (as are all the other dollar figures I am about to give you). Thirty-five percent of adults in those four census tracts had bachelor's degrees or higher— or to think of it another way, almost two out of three adults in Austin's most affluent neighborhoods did *not* have a college education.

Fast forward to the census of 2000. The population had grown to 657,000, making Austin the sixteenth largest city in the nation. The wealthy still live to the West of downtown, but those neighborhoods now house a different demographic than they had forty years earlier. In 2000, the median income in the richest of Austin's zip codes was $209,000, and several others had median family incomes of more than $100,000.

Education levels had risen as much as income. In 1960, the highest proportion of adults with college degrees was just 39 percent in any census tract in the city. In 2000, a dozen zip codes were above 60 percent.

Instead of being a sleepy city, Austin had become home to some of the trendiest and highest tech industries in the country. Dell Computer has its headquarters in Austin. So does Whole Foods Market. A partial list of new-economy companies that had located some of their operations in Austin then or in the decade to follow includes Apple, Google, Freescale Semiconductor, Cirrus Logic, lots of other information technology companies, and 85 biotechnology companies.

Those kinds of employers mean a lot of employees who not only have BAs, but really high IQs. Many were graduates of elite universities. And the culture was transformed. To the rest of Texas, Austin became known as "the People's Republic of Austin" because of the lefty tilt of the new elite who had displaced the Texas good-old-boys who had once headed most of Austin's affluent families.

Seventeen hundred miles to the northeast and a world away from Austin is Manhattan. Then as now, the richest part of Manhattan is the Upper East Side, extending from Fifth Avenue to the East River between 59th Street and 96th Streets. To some degree, it was already a world apart in 1960. In the census tracts that bordered Fifth Avenue, median family incomes were more than $150,000. But even in those wealthiest of all census tracts anywhere in the nation, only a third of the adults were college-educated. In the Upper East Side as a whole, just 24 percent of adults had college degrees. The median family income for the Upper East Side as a whole? $84,000. In 2010 dollars. That is less than the current salary of an experienced teacher in the New York public school system.

Fast forward to the 2000 census. Like Austin, Manhattan has been transformed. In 1960, about 47 percent of the jobs of people who lived in Manhattan were blue-collar. By 2000, that had fallen to 8 percent, and almost everyone who held such jobs lived north of Central Park, in Harlem. In the Upper East Side itself, the median family income had risen from the $84,000 of 1960 to $180,000. The proportion of adults with college degrees had risen from 24 percent to 75 percent. In the rest of Manhattan south of 96th street, as of 2000 the median income is over $100,000. The proportion of adults with college degrees had risen from about 15 percent to more than 65 percent. Except for Harlem, Manhattan had turned into the abode for a highly educated, highly paid professional, managerial, and technical class.

The third city is not really a city. Eleven hundred miles west of Manhattan, and another world away, is Newton, Iowa. In 1960, the census listed Newton's population as 15,381. It was the home of the Maytag Company, the washing machine manufacturer, which ranked to two-tenths of one percent of American families. The authentically wealthy in 1960 comprised a microscopic fraction of the population.

Beginning in the 1980s, as the baby boomers began to reach maturity, that critical mass developed, driven by a variety of factors that I will not try to discuss now. The point is that a separate elite culture did develop.

The new elite culture pervades every aspect of life. If you want to get a quick sense of just how visibly different the new upper class is from mainstream America, attend a parents' night at an elementary school in a working- or middle-class neighborhood, and then attend parents' night at an elite private elementary school.

It starts in the parking lot. In the parking lot of the ordinary school, most of the cars will be American brands; at the elite private school, the overwhelming majority will be foreign. Then notice the age of the parents. In the mainstream school, the mothers of the children are mostly in their late twenties to mid-thirties. In the elite school, you may see no mothers at all who are in their twenties, but you will see many who are in their forties. With fathers are even older.

There is a difference in weight. In the mainstream school, two-thirds of the parents are overweight and about one-third are obese (proportions that are consistent with the national distribution from the 2009 survey of obesity by the National Center for Health Statistics). At the elite private school, the parents are, on average, a lot thinner. They may work out at their health club and be attractively lean or run marathons and look emaciated, but they are seldom fat.

The members of the new upper class are healthy in other ways. They know their cholesterol count and often their percentage of body fat. They eat lots of whole grains, green vegetables, and olive oil. They aren't big drinkers, usually confining themselves to wine or boutique beers. As for smoking, do not try to light up when you visit an upper-class home unless you want to become an instant social pariah.

The new upper class doesn't read the same newspapers or watch the same television shows as mainstream America. Liberal members of the new upper class check the *New York Times* every day no matter where they live, while conservative members of the new upper class check *The Wall Street Journal* every day no matter where they live. Many don't bother to read the local newspaper, and they wouldn't be caught of their actions; that it is not the government's job to protect people from themselves; that it is not the government's job to stage-manage how people interact with each other. Discard the system that created the cultural capital, and the qualities we love about Americans can go away. In some circles, they are going away.

We have a problem at both the bottom and the top of American society. And since it is the top that has such decisive influence on American culture, economy, and governance, it is the top that has to take the lead in confronting their increasing isolation.

I am not suggesting that the people of Belmont sacrifice their own self-interest for everyone else. That would be really un-American. I just want to accelerate a rediscovery of what that self-interest is. Age-old human wisdom has understood that a life well-lived requires engagement with those around us. That is reality, not idealism. It is appropriate to think that a political Great Awakening in Belmont can arise in part from the renewed understanding that it can be pleasant to lead a glossy life, but it is ultimately more fun to lead a textured life, and to be in the midst of others who are leading textured lives.

Belmont parents have to ask tough questions of themselves about what is really the best environment for their children. Do they really want to raise hot-house flowers, protected all their lives from everything sweaty and troublesome? The children of Belmont need to ask themselves what they can do to break out of the bubble, and to learn what it is like to live in mainstream America. Belmont employers need to ask what kind of people they really want to fill their managerial openings. Do they want to go for the brightest of the bright from Harvard, Princeton, and Yale, or should they be looking for other qualities that are more likely to be found elsewhere?

The motivation for asking these questions, and finding answers to them, has nothing to do with the day-to-day issues of public policy. They have everything to do with why America is exceptional, and why it is so important that America remain exceptional. They have everything to do with what lies at the core of the American project: a different way for people to live together, unique among the nations of the earth, and immeasurably precious.

LUDWIG VON MISES

EXCERPTS FROM

PLANNING FOR FREEDOM

Economic Teaching at the Universities

This article appeared in The Freeman, *April 7, 1952.*

A few years ago a House of Representatives Subcommittee on Publicity and Propaganda in the Executive Departments, under the chairmanship of Representative Forest A. Harness, investigated Federal propaganda operations. On one occasion the Committee had as a witness a government-employed doctor. When asked if his public speeches throughout the country presented both sides of the discussion touching compulsory national health insurance, this witness answered: "I don't know what you mean by both sides."

This naive answer throws light on the state of mind of people who proudly call themselves progressive intellectuals. They simply do not imagine that any argument could be advanced against the various schemes they are suggesting. As they see it, everybody, without asking questions, must support every project aiming at more and more government control of all aspects of the citizen's life and conduct. They never try to refute the objections raised against their doctrines. They prefer, as Mrs. Eleanor Roosevelt recently did in her column, to call dishonest those with whom they do not agree.

Ludwig von Mises, *Planning for Freedom; and Twelve other Essays and Addresses* (South Holland, IN: Libertarian Press, 1974), pp. 161–72, 173–79, 180–84. See also the Ludwig von Mises Institute—http://mises.org.

Many eminent citizens hold educational institutions responsible for the spread of this bigotry. They sharply criticize the way in which economics, philosophy, sociology, history and political science are taught at most American universities and colleges. They blame many teachers for indoctrinating their students with the ideas of all-round planning, socialism and communism. Some of those attacked try to deny any responsibility. Others, realizing that the futility of this mode of defense, cry out about "persecution" and infringement of "academic freedom."

Yet what is unsatisfactory with present-day academic conditions— not only in this country but in most foreign nations—is not the fact that many teachers are blindly committed to Veblenian, Marxian and Keynesian fallacies, and try to convince their students that no tenable objections can be raised against what they call progressive policies. The mischief is rather to be seen in the fact that the statements of these teachers are not challenged by any criticism in the academic sphere. The pseudo-liberals monopolize the teaching jobs at many universities. Only men who agree with them are appointed as teachers and instructors of the social sciences, and only textbooks supporting their ideas are used. The essential question is not how to get rid of inept teachers and poor textbooks. It is how to give the students an opportunity to hear something about the ideas of economists rejecting the tenets of the interventionists, inflationists, Socialists and Communists.

1. Methods of the "Progressive" Teachers

Let us illustrate the matter by reviewing a recently published book. A professor of Harvard University edits, with the support of an advisory committee whose members are all like himself professors of economics at Harvard University, a series of textbooks, the "Economics Handbook Series." In this series there was published a volume on socialism. Its author, Paul M. Sweezy, opens his preface with the declaration that the book "is written from the standpoint of a Socialist." The editor of the series, Professor Seymour E. Harris, in his introduction goes a step further in stating that the author's viewpoint is nearer that of the group which determines Soviet policy than the one which now [1949] holds the reins of government in Britain." This is a mild description of the facts that the volume is from the first to the last page an uncritical eulogy of the Soviet system.

Now it is perfectly legitimate for Dr. Sweezy to write such a book and for the professors to edit and to publish it. The United States is a free country—one of the few free countries left in the world—and the Constitution and its amendments grant to everybody the right to think as he likes and to have published in print what he thinks. Sweezy has in fact unwittingly rendered a great service to the discerning public. For his volume clearly shows to every judicious reader conversant with economics that the most eminent advocates of socialism are at their wits' end, do not know how to advance any plausible argument in favor of their creed, and are utterly at a loss to refute any of the serious objections raised against it.

But the book is not designed for perspicacious scholars well acquainted with the social sciences. It is, as the editors' introduction emphasizes, written for the general reader in order to popularize ideas, and especially also for use in the classroom. Laymen and students who know nothing or very little about the problems involved will draw all their knowledge about socialism from it. They lack the familiarity with theories and facts which would enable them to form an independent opinion about the various doctrines expounded by the author. They will accept all his theses and descriptions as incontestable science and wisdom. How could they be so presumptuous as to doubt the reliability of a book, written, as the introduction says, by an "authority" in the field and sponsored by a committee of professors of venerable Harvard!

The shortcoming of the committee is not to be seen in the fact that they have published such a book, but in the fact that their series contains only this book about socialism. If they had, together with Dr. Sweezy's book, published another volume critically analyzing communist ideas and the achievements of socialist governments, nobody could blame them for disseminating communism. Decency should have impelled them to give the critics of socialism and communism the same chance to represent their views to the students of universities and colleges as they gave to Dr. Sweezy.

On every page of Dr. Sweezy's book one finds really amazing statements. Thus, in dealing with the problem of civil rights under a

socialist regime, he simply equates the Soviet Constitution with the
American Constitution. Both, he declares, are

> generally accepted as the statement of the ideals which ought
> to guide the actions of both the state and the individual
> citizen. That these ideals are not always lived up to—either
> in the Soviet Union or in the United States—is certainly both
> true and important; but it does not mean that they do not
> exist or that they can be ignored, still less that they can be
> transformed into their opposite.

Leaving aside most of what could be advanced to explode this
reasoning, there is need to realize that the American Constitution is
not merely an ideal but the valid law of the country. To prevent it from
becoming a dead letter there is an independent judiciary culminating
in the Supreme Court. Without such a guardian of law and legality any
law can be and is ignored and transformed into its opposite. Did Dr.
Sweezy never become aware of this nuance? Does he really believe that
the millions languishing in Soviet prisons and labor camps can invoke
habeas corpus?

To say it again: Dr. Sweezy has the right—precisely because the
American Bill of Rights is not merely an ideal, but an enforced law—to
transform every fact into its opposite. But professors who hand out such
praise of the Soviets to their students without informing them about the
opinions of the opponents of socialism must not raise the cry of witch-
hunt if they are criticized.

Professor Harris in his introduction contends that "those who
fear undue influence of the present volume may be cheered by a
forthcoming companion volume on capitalism in this series written by
one as devoted to private enterprise as Dr. Sweezy is to socialism." This
volume, written by Professor David McCord Wright of the University
of Virginia, has been published in the meantime. It deals incidentally
also with socialism and tries to explode some minor socialist fallacies,
such as the doctrine of the withering away of the State, a doctrine which
even the most fanatical Soviet authors relegate today to an insignificant
position. But it certainly can not be considered a satisfactory substitute,
or a substitute at all, for a thoroughly critical examination of the whole

body of socialist and communist ideas and the lamentable failure of all socialist experiments. Some of the teachers try to refute the accusations of ideological intolerance leveled against their universities and to demonstrate their own impartiality by occasionally inviting a dissenting outsider to address their students. This is mere eyewash. One hour of sound economics against several years of indoctrination of errors! The present writer may quote from a letter in which he declined such an invitation:

> What makes it impossible for me to present the operation of the market economy in a short lecture—whether fifty minutes or twice fifty minutes—is the fact that people, influenced by the prevailing ideas on economic problems, are full of erroneous opinions concerning this system. They are convinced that economic depressions, mass unemployment, monopoly, aggressive imperialism and wars, and the poverty of the greater part of mankind, are caused by the unhampered operation of the capitalist mode of production.
>
> If a lecturer does not dispel each of these dogmas, the impression left with the audience is unsatisfactory. Now, exploding any one of them requires much more time than that assigned to me in your program. The hearers will think: "He did not refer at all to this" or "He made only a few casual remarks about that." My lecture would rather confirm them in their misunderstanding of the system.... If it were possible to expound the operation of capitalism in one or two short addresses, it would be a waste of time to keep the students of economics for several years at the universities. It would be difficult to explain why voluminous textbooks have to be written about this subject.... It is these reasons that impel me reluctantly to decline your kind invitation.

2. The Alleged Impartiality of the Universities

The pseudo-progressive teachers excuse their policy of barring all those whom they smear as old-fashioned reactionaries from access to teaching positions by calling these men biased.

The reference to bias is quite out of place if the accuser is not in a position to demonstrate clearly in what the deficiency of the smeared author's doctrine consists. The only thing that matters is whether a doctrine is sound or unsound. This is to be established by facts and deductive reasoning. If no tenable arguments can be advanced to invalidate a theory, it does not in the least detract from its correctness if the author is called names. If, on the other hand, the falsity of a doctrine has already been clearly demonstrated by an irrefutable chain of reasoning, there is no need to call its author biased.

A biographer may try to explain the manifestly exploded errors of the person whose life he is writing about by tracing them back to bias. But such psychological interpretation is immaterial in discussions concerning the correctness or falsity of a theory. Professors who call those with whom they disagree biased merely confess their inability to discover any fault in their adversaries' theories.

Many "progressive" professors have for some time served in one of the various alphabetical government agencies. The tasks entrusted to them in the bureaus were as a rule ancillary only. They compiled statistics and wrote memoranda which their superiors, either politicians or former managers of corporations, filed without reading. The professors did not instill a scientific spirit into the bureaus. But the bureaus gave them the mentality of authoritarianism. They distrust the populace and consider the State (with a capital S) as the God-sent guardian of the wretched underlings. Only the Government is impartial and unbiased. Whoever opposes any expansion of governmental powers is by this token unmasked as an enemy of the commonweal. It is manifest that he "hates" the State.

Now if an economist is opposed to the socialization of industries, he does not "hate" the State. He simply declares that the commonwealth is better served by private ownership of the means of production than by public ownership. Nobody could pretend that experience with nationalized enterprises contradicts this opinion.

Another typically bureaucratic prejudice which the professors acquired in Washington is to call the attitudes of those opposing government controls and the establishment of new offices "negativism." In the light of this terminology all that has been achieved by the

American individual enterprise system is only "negative"; the bureaus alone are "positive."

There is, furthermore, the spurious antithesis "plan or no plan." Only totalitarian government planning that reduces the citizens to mere pawns in the designs of the bureaucracy is called planning. The plans of the individual citizens are simply "no plans." What semantics!

3. How Modern History is Taught

The progressive intellectual looks upon capitalism as the most ghastly of all evils. Mankind, he contends, lived rather happily in the good old days. But then, as a British historian said, the Industrial Revolution "fell like a war or a plague" on the peoples. The "bourgeoisie" converted plenty into scarcity. A few tycoons enjoy all luxuries. But, as Marx himself observed, the worker "sinks deeper and deeper" because the bourgeoisie "is incompetent to assure an existence to its slave within his slavery."

Still worse are the intellectual and moral effects of the capitalist mode of production. There is but one means, the progressive believes, to free mankind from the misery and degradation produced by laissez-faire and rugged individualism, *viz.*, to adopt central planning, the system with which the Russians are successfully experimenting. It is true that the results obtained by the Soviets are not yet fully satisfactory. But these shortcomings were caused only by the peculiar conditions of Russia. The West will avoid the pitfalls of the Russians and will realize the Welfare State without the merely accidental features that disfigured it in Russia and in Hitler Germany.

Such is the philosophy taught at most present-day schools and propagated by novels and plays. It is this doctrine that guides the actions of almost all contemporary governments. The American "progressive" feels ashamed of what he calls the social backwardness of his country. He considers it a duty of the United States to subsidize foreign socialist governments lavishly in order to enable them to go on with their ruinous socialist ventures. In his eyes the real enemy of the American people is Big Business, that is, the enterprises which provide the American common man with the highest standard of living ever reached in history. He hails every step forward on the road toward all-round control of business as progress. He smears all those who hint at the pernicious effects of waste, deficit spending and capital decumulation as reactionaries, economic royalists and Fascists. He never mentions the new or improved products which business almost every year makes accessible to the masses. But he goes into raptures about the rather questionable achievements of the Tennessee Valley Authority, the deficit of which is made good out of taxes collected from Big Business.

The most infatuated expositors of this ideology are to be found in the university departments of history, political science, sociology and literature. The professors of these departments enjoy the advantage, in referring to economic issues, that they are talking about a subject with which they are not familiar at all. This is especially flagrant in the case of historians. The way in which the history of the last two hundred years has been treated is really a scandal. Only recently eminent scholars have begun to unmask the crude fallacies of Lujo Brentano, the Webbs, the Hammonds, Tawney, Arnold Toynbee, Elie Halévy, the Beards and other authors. At the last meeting of the Mont Pèlerin Society the occupant of the chair of economic history at the London School of Economics, Professor T. S. Ashton, presented a paper in which he pointed out that the commonly accepted views of the economic developments of the nineteenth century "are not informed by any glimmering of economic sense." The historians tortured the facts when they concocted the legend that "the dominant form of organization under industrial capitalism, the factory, arose out of the demands, not of ordinary people, but of the rich and the rulers."

The truth is that the characteristic feature of capitalism was and is mass production for the needs of the masses. Whenever the factory with its methods of mass production by means of power-driven machines invaded a new branch of production, it started with cheap goods for the broad masses. The factories turned to the production of more refined and therefore more expensive merchandise only at a later stage, when the unprecedented improvement which they had caused in the masses' standard of living made it reasonable to apply the methods of mass production to better articles as well. Big business caters to the needs of the many; it depends exclusively upon mass consumption. In his capacity as consumer the common man is the sovereign whose buying or abstention from buying decides the fate of entrepreneurial activities. The "proletarian" is the much-talked-about customer who is *always* right.

The most popular method of deprecating capitalism is to make it responsible for every condition which is considered unsatisfactory. Tuberculosis, and, until a few years ago, syphilis, were called diseases of capitalism. The destitution of scores of millions in countries like India, which did *not* adopt capitalism, is blamed on capitalism. It is a sad fact that people become debilitated in old age and finally die. But this happens not only to salesmen but also to employers, and it was no less tragic in the pre-capitalistic ages than it is under capitalism. Prostitution, dipsomania and drug addiction are all called capitalist vices.

Whenever people discuss the alleged misdeed of the capitalists, a learned professor or a sophisticated artist refers to the high income of movie stars, boxers and wrestlers. But who contributes more to these incomes, the millionaires, or the "proletarians"?

It must be admitted that the worst excesses in this propaganda are not committed by professors economics but by the teachers of the other social sciences, by journalists, writers and sometimes even by ministers. But the source from which all the slogans of this hectic fanaticism spring is the teachings handed down by the "institutionalist" school of economic policies. All these dogmas and fallacies can be ultimately traced back to allegedly economic doctrines.

4. The Proscription of Sound Economics

The Marxians, Keynesians, Veblenians and other "progressives" know very well that their doctrines can not stand any critical analysis. They are fully aware of the fact that one representative of sound economics in their department would nullify all their teachings. This is why they are so anxious to bar every "orthodox" from access to the strongholds of their "un-orthodoxy."

The worst consequence of this proscription of sound economics is the fact that gifted young graduates shun the career of an academic economist. They do not want to be boycotted by universities, book reviewers and publishing firms. They prefer to go into business or the practice of law, where their talents will be fairly appreciated. It is mainly compromisers, who are not eager to find out the shortcomings of the official doctrine, who aspire to the teaching positions. There are few competent men left to take the place of the eminent scholars who die or reach the retirement age. Among the rising generation of instructors are hardly any worthy successors of such economists at Frank A. Fetter and Edwin W. Kemmerer of Princeton, Irving Fisher of Yale and Benjamin M. Anderson of California.

There is but one way to remedy this situation. True economists must be given the same opportunity in our faculties which only the advocates of socialism and interventionism enjoy today. This is surely not too much to ask as long as this country has not yet gone totalitarian.

• • • •

Trends Can Change

This article appeared in The Freeman, *April 12, 1951.*

One of the cherished dogmas implied in contemporary fashionable doctrines is the belief that tendencies of social evolution as manifested in the recent past will prevail in the future too. Study of the past, it is assumed, discloses the shape of things to come. Any attempt to reverse or even to stop a trend is doomed to failure. Man must submit to the irresistible power of historical destiny.

To this dogma is added the Hegelian idea of progressive improvement in human conditions. Every later stage of history, Hegel taught, is of necessity a higher and more perfect state than the preceding one, is progress toward the ultimate goal which God in his infinite goodness set for mankind. Thus any doubt with regard to the excellence of what is bound to come is unwarranted, unscientific and blasphemous. Those fighting "progress" are not only committed to a hopeless venture. They are also morally wicked, *reactionary*, for they want to prevent the emergence of conditions that will benefit the immense majority.

From the point of view of this philosophy its adepts, the self-styled "progressives," deal with the fundamental issues of economic policies. They do not examine the merits and demerits of suggested measures and reforms. This would, in their eyes, be unscientific. As they see it, the only question that has to be answered is whether such proposed innovations do or do not agree with the spirit of our age and follow the direction which destiny has ordained for the course of human affairs. The drift of the policies of the recent past teaches us what is both inescapable and beneficial. The only legitimate source for the cognition of what is salutary and has to be accomplished today is the knowledge of what was accomplished yesterday.

In the last decades there prevailed a trend toward more and more government interference with business. The sphere of the private citizen's initiative was narrowed down. Laws and administrative decrees restricted the field in which entrepreneurs and capitalists were free to conduct their activities in compliance with the wishes of the consumers as manifested in the structure of the market. From year to year an ever-increasing portion of profits and interest on capital invested was confiscated by taxation of corporation earnings and individual incomes and estates. "Social" control, i.e., government control, of business is step by step substituted for private control. The "progressives" are certain that this trend toward wresting "economic" power from the parasitic "leisure class" and its transfer to "the people" will go on until the "welfare state" will have supplanted the nefarious capitalistic system which history has doomed forever. Notwithstanding sinister machinations on the part of "the interests," mankind, led by government economists and other bureaucrats, politicians and union bosses, marches steadily toward the bliss of an earthly paradise.

The prestige of this myth is so enormous that it quells any opposition. It spreads defeatism among those who do not share the opinion that everything which comes later is better than what preceded, and are fully aware of the disastrous effects of all-round planning, i.e., totalitarian socialism. They, too, meekly submit to what, the pseudo-scholars tell them, is inevitable. It is this mentality of passively accepting defeat that has made socialism triumph in many European countries and may very soon make it conquer in this country too.

The Marxian dogma of the inevitability of socialism was based on the thesis that capitalism necessarily results in progressive impoverishment of the immense majority of people. All the advantages of technological progress benefit exclusively the small minority of exploiters. The masses are condemned to increasing "misery, oppression, slavery, degradation, exploitation." No action on the part of governments or labor unions can succeed in stopping this evolution. Only socialism, which is bound to come "with the inexorability of a law of nature," will bring salvation by "the expropriation of the few usurpers by the mass of people."

Facts have belied this prognosis no less than all other Marxian forecasts. In the capitalist countries the common man's standard of living is today incomparably higher than it was in the days of Marx. It is simply not true that the fruits of technological improvement are enjoyed exclusively by the capitalists while the laborer, as the Communist Manifesto says, "instead of rising with the progress of industry, sinks deeper and deeper." Not a minority of "rugged individualists," but the masses, are the main consumers of the products turned out by large-scale production. Only morons can still cling to the fable that capitalism "is incompetent to assure an existence to its slave within his slavery."

Today the doctrine of the irreversibility of prevailing trends has supplanted the Marxian doctrine concerning the inevitability of progressive impoverishment.

Now this doctrine is devoid of any logical or experimental verification. Historical trends do not necessarily go on forever. No practical man is so foolish as to assume that prices will keep rising because the price curves of the past show an upward tendency. On the contrary, the more prices soar, the more alarmed cautious businessmen become about a possible reversal. Almost all prognostications which our government statisticians made on the basis of their study of the figures available—which necessarily always refer to the past—have proved faulty. What is called extrapolation of trend lines is viewed by sound statistical theory with the utmost suspicion.

The same refers also to developments in fields which are not open to description by statistical figures. There was, for instance, in the course of ancient Greco-Roman civilization a tendency toward an interregional division of labor. The trade between the various parts of the vast Roman Empire intensified more and more. But then came a turning-point. Commerce declined and there finally emerged the medieval manor system, with almost complete autarky of every landowner's household.

Or, to quote another example, there prevailed in the eighteenth century a tendency toward reducing the severity and the horrors of war. In 1770 the Comte de Guibert could write: "Today the whole of Europe is civilized. Wars have become less cruel. Except in combat no blood is shed; prisoners are respected; towns are no longer destroyed; the country is no more ravaged."

Can anybody maintain that this trend has not been changed?

But even if it were true that an historical trend must go on forever, and that therefore the coming of socialism is inevitable, it would still not be permissible to infer that socialism will be a better, or even more than that, the most perfect state of society's economic organization. There is nothing to support such a conclusion other than the arbitrary pseudo-theological surmises of Hegel, Comte and Marx, according to which every later stage of the historical process must be necessarily be a better state. It is not true that human conditions must always improve, and that a relapse into very unsatisfactory modes of life, penury and barbarism is impossible. The comparatively high standard of living which the common man enjoys today in the capitalist countries is an achievement of laissez-faire capitalism. Neither theoretical reasoning nor historical experience allows the inference that it could be preserved, still less be improved under socialism.

In the last decades in many countries the number of divorces and of suicides has increased from year to year. Yet hardly anybody will have the temerity to contend that this trend means progress toward more satisfactory conditions.

The typical graduate of colleges and high schools very soon forgets most of the things he has learned. But there is one piece of indoctrination which makes a lasting impression on his mind, *viz.*, the dogma of the irreversibility of the trend toward all-round planning and regimentation. He does not doubt the thesis that mankind will never return to capitalism, the dismal system of an age gone forever, and that the "wave of the future" carries us toward the promised land of Cockaigne. If he had any doubts, what he reads in newspapers and what he hears from the politicians would dispel them. For even the candidates nominated by the parties of opposition, although critical of the measures of the party in power, protest that they are not "reactionary," and do not venture to stop the march toward "progress."

Thus the average man is predisposed in favor of socialism. Of course, he does not approve of everything that the Soviets have done. He thinks that the Russians have blundered in many respects, and he excuses these errors as being caused by their unfamiliarity with freedom. He blames the leaders, especially Stalin, for the corruption of the lofty ideal of all-round planning. His sympathies go rather to Tito, the upright rebel, who refuses to surrender to Russia. Not so long ago he displayed the same friendly feelings for Benes, and until only a few months ago for Mao Tse-tung, the "agrarian reformer."

At any rate, a good part of American public opinion believes that this country is in essential matters backward, as it has not yet, like the Russians, wiped out production for profit and unemployment and has not yet attained stability. Practically nobody thinks that he could learn something important about these problems from a serious occupation with economics. The dogmas of the irreversibility of prevailing tendencies and of their unfailingly beneficial effects render such studies supererogatory. If economics confirms these dogmas, it is superfluous; if it is at variance with them, it is illusory and deceptive.

Now trends of evolution can change, and hitherto they almost always have changed. But they changed only because they met firm opposition. The prevailing trend toward what Hilaire Belloc called the servile state will certainly not be reversed if nobody has the courage to attack its underlying dogmas.

• • • •

The Political Chances of
Genuine Liberalism
This article was first printed in Farmand, *February 17, 1951 (Oslo, Norway).*

The outlook of many eminent champions of genuine liberalism is rather pessimistic today. As they see it, the vitriolic slogans of the socialists and interventionists call forth a better response from the masses than the cool reasoning of judicious men. The majority of the voters are just dull and mentally inert people who dislike thinking and are easily deceived by the enticing promises of irresponsible pied pipers. Subconscious inferiority complexes and envy push people toward the parties of the left. They rejoice in the policies of confiscating the greater part of the income and wealth of successful businessmen without grasping the fact that these policies harm their own material interests. Disregarding all the objections raised by economists, they firmly believe that they can get many good things for nothing. Even in the United States people, although enjoying the highest standard of living ever attained in history, are prepared to condemn capitalism as a vile economy of scarcity and to indulge in day dreams about an economy of abundance in which everybody will get everything "according to his needs." The case for freedom and material prosperity is hopeless. The future belongs to the demagogues who know nothing else than to dissipate the capital accumulated by previous generations. Mankind is plunging into a return to the dark ages. Western civilization is doomed.

The main error of this widespread pessimism is the belief that the destructionist ideas and policies of our age sprang from the proletarians and are a "revolt of the masses." In fact, the masses, precisely because they are not creative and do not develop philosophies of their own, follow the leaders. The ideologies which produced all the mischiefs and catastrophes of our century are not an achievement of the mob. They are the feat of pseudo-scholars and pseudo-intellectuals. They were propagated from the chairs of universities and from the pulpit, they were disseminated by the press, by novels and plays and by the movies and the radio. The intellectuals converted the masses to socialism and interventionism. These ideologies owe the power they have today to the fact that all means of communication have been turned over to their supporters and almost all dissenters have been virtually silenced. What is needed to turn the flood is to change the mentality of the intellectuals. Then the masses will follow suit.

Furthermore it is not true that the ideas of genuine liberalism are too complicated to appeal to the untutored mind of the average voter. It is not a hopeless task to explain to the wage earners that the only means to raise wage rates *for all those eager to find jobs and to earn wages* is to increase the per head quota of capital invested. The pessimists underrate the mental abilities of the "common man" when they assert that he cannot grasp the disastrous consequences of policies resulting in capital decumulation. Why do all "underdeveloped countries" ask for American aid and American capital? Why do they not rather expect aid from socialist Russia?

The acme of the policies of all self-styled progressive parties and governments is to raise artificially the prices of vital commodities above the height they would have attained on the markets of unhampered laissez-faire capitalism. Only an infinitesimal fraction of the American people is interested in the preservation of a high price for sugar. The immense majority of the American voters are buyers and consumers, not producers and sellers of sugar. Nonetheless the American Government is firmly committed to a policy of high sugar prices by rigorously restricting both the importation of sugar from abroad and domestic production. Similar policies are adopted with regard to the prices of bread, meat, butter, eggs, potatoes, cotton and many other agricultural products. It is a serious blunder to call this procedure indiscriminately a pro-farmers policy. Less than one-fifth of the United States' total population are dependent upon agriculture for a living. Yet the interests of these people with regard to the prices of various agricultural products are not identical. The dairyman is not interested in a high, but in a low price for wheat, fodder, sugar and cotton. The owners of chicken farms are hurt by high prices of any agricultural product but chickens and eggs. It is obvious that the growers of cotton, grapes, oranges, apples, grapefruit and cranberries are prejudiced by a system which raises the prices of staple foods. Most of the items of the so-called pro-farm policy favor only a minority of the total farming population at the expense of the majority not only of the non-farming, but also of the farming population.

Things are hardly different in other fields. When the railroadmen or the workers of the building trades, supported by laws and administrative practises which are admittedly loaded against their employers, indulge in feather-bedding and other devices allegedly destined to "create more jobs," they are unfairly fleecing the immense majority of their fellow-citizens. The unions of the printers enhance the prices of books and periodicals and thus affect all people eager to read and to learn. The so-called pro-labor policies bring about a state of affairs under which each group of wage earners is intent upon improving their own conditions at the expense of the consumers, *viz.*, the enormous majority.

Nobody knows today whether he wins more from those policies which are favoring the group to which he himself belongs than he loses on account of the policies which favor all the other groups. But it is certain that all are adversely affected by the general drop in the productivity of industrial effort and output which these allegedly beneficial policies inevitably bring about.

Until a few years ago the advocates of these unsuitable policies tried to defend them by pointing out that their incidence reduces only the wealth and income of the rich and benefits the masses at the sole expense of useless parasites. There is no need to explode the fallacies of this reasoning. Even if we admit its conclusiveness for the sake of argument, we must realize that, with the exception of a few countries, this "surplus" fund of the rich has already been exhausted. Even Mr. Hugh Gaitskell, Sir Stafford Cripps' successor as the *Führer* of Great Britain's economy, could not help declaring that "there is not enough money to take away from England's rich to raise standards of living any further." In the United States the policy of "soaking the rich" has not yet gone so far as that. But if the trend of American politics is not entirely reversed very soon, this richest of all countries will have to face the same situation in a few years.

Conditions being such, the prospects for a genuinely liberal revival may appear propitious. At least fifty per cent of the voters are women, most of them housewives or prospective housewives. To the common sense of these women a program of low prices will make a strong appeal. They will certainly cast their ballot for candidates who proclaim: Do away peremptorily will all policies and measures destined to enhance prices above the height of the unhampered market! Do away with all this dismal stuff of price supports, parity prices, tariffs and quotas, intergovernmental commodity control agreements and so on! Abstain from increasing the quantity of money in circulation and from credit expansion, from all illusory attempts to lower the rate of interest and from deficit spending! What we want is low prices.

In the end these judicious householders will even succeed in convincing their husbands.

In the *Communist Manifesto* Karl Marx and Frederick Engels asserted: "The cheap prices of its commodities are the heavy artillery with which capitalism batters down all Chinese walls." We may hope that these cheap prices will also batter down the highest of all Chinese walls, *viz.*, those erected by the folly of bad economic policies.

To express such hopes is not merely wishful thinking.

• • • •